The Man in the Garlic Tuxedo

MIKE KENNY

GARLIC PRESS

MIKE KENNY

© 2014 Mike Kenny. All rights reserved. No part of this book may be reproduced or transmitted in any form or by any means, electronic or mechanical, including photocopying, recording, or by any information storage and retrieval system, without written permission from the author, except for the inclusion of brief quotations in a review.

Printed in the United States of America.

Garlic Press
Peoria, Arizona

Trade Paperback 978-0-991-51640-7

Cover design by Mark Korsak
Book design by Catherine Leonardo

This edition was prepared for printing by The Editorial Department
7650 E. Broadway, #308, Tucson, Arizona 85710
www.editorialdepartment.com

PUBLISHER'S NOTE: This is a work of nonfiction; however, certain names, places, and dates have been altered.

Contents

SECTION ONE
What I Heard *1*

CHAPTERS
In the Beginning *3*
Italy *7*
South Africa *19*
England *23*
Brooklyn *27*
Pennsylvania *51*
New Jersey *59*

SECTION TWO
What I Know *63*

CHAPTERS
The Chef *67*
The Communicator *81*
The Negotiator *87*

Contents

The Businessman *113*
The Hipster *121*
The Handyman *127*
The Beast *133*
The Great Communicator *139*
The Family Man *145*
Arizona *153*
Babbo *161*
The Giver *165*
The Doctor *171*
The Patient *177*
The Artist *183*
The Safekeeper *189*
The Man in the Garlic Tuxedo *193*
The Greatest Communicator *207*
The Philosopher *229*
The Tough Mudder *235*
The Enigma *239*
The Environmentalist *243*
Mr. Self-Aware *247*
Babbo Part Two *251*
My Father-in-Law *255*
Acknowledgements *259*

What I Heard

In the Beginning

*From dust and His own breath, the Lord created Adam.
And many years later, when a great descendant emerged,
gasping, the Lord sayeth, "Thou shalt stick a
chicken beak in his buttocks."*

— not the Bible

In 1947, in the Italian region of Calabria, in the small town of Siderno, a boy was born.

This boy was born in a house as opposed to a hospital, by a midwife as opposed to a doctor, because back in the day they kept it real. Especially in Siderno, which had only zero hospitals, and the only way to get to a hospital was to ride your donkey into Rome, which took eight years. There was no time for that.

The delivery was a success, unless you count the fact that the boy was not breathing. He was turning blue, deprived of oxygen.

The midwife thought maybe he was choking, so she held the boy upside down as a means to remove the obstruction.

The Man in the Garlic Tuxedo

This did not work. Everybody was, as they say in Italian, straight trippin'.

Time was running out, but the midwife had an idea. She screamed, "Vai a prendere un pollo da zi Rosina!"

This means, obviously if you consider context, "Go get a chicken from Rosina!" Rosina was the neighbor. She had chickens. By the way, almost everyone in Calabria at the time owned a bunch of chickens, and other animals, and a farm probably, and grew their own cheese. It was no biggie to be readily available to grab a live chicken at any given moment. "Get a chicken" in Calabria in the 1940s is the equivalent of saying "Please pass the potato chips" in present-day America.

So anyway, someone went and got a chicken from Rosina's backyard. The midwife took the chicken and did the only sensible thing a person can do in such a situation: She stuck the chicken's beak right up the baby boy's butt. The thought process behind this was that the breath from the chicken would travel up the baby's anus, directly into the lungs (biology 101). Without access to a wind-generating module containing a point tiny enough to enter a newborn child, the beak of a live, breathing fowl would suffice.

I like to believe the last thing that went through that chicken's mind was "Here goes nothing!"

It worked. Breath was returned to the boy's lungs, and everyone else exhaled as well. Except, that is, the chicken, which did not make it. It was a sacrifice any family would make, albeit one that few families would be aware they *could* make under those circumstances.

The midwife said, "Il bambino e salvato. Il pollo e morto."

In the Beginning

This means simply that the baby was saved, and the chicken died, but implies that the sickness or bad spirit of the choking child had transferred from the boy to the chicken, killing it and saving a human life. In the Bible, Jesus removes demons from a man and sends them into a herd of pigs, which promptly run off a cliff. Let us then conclude that animals are totally *not* the beneficiaries of the removal of bad spirits. That is not the thesis of this book, but warrants mention.

Although modern medicine and science may be unable to account for what happened that day, I suppose it's possible that air was literally breathed into the body, resuscitating the child. It's also possible the pure shock of having a chicken in his ass awoke the baby out of his stupor. That would certainly do it for me. Regardless of the process, the miraculous result does honor the ancient axiom "Never underestimate an Italian midwife with a plan."

The reason many of our close-knit group of family and friends are here today, either physically or in our present position in life, is thanks to that brave chicken and the man it saved. I think the chicken would be very proud to know about the man for whom it sacrificed its life. They named him Antonio, and he went on to see the world, leaving the region of Calabria for, eventually, America, where he became just the 1,272,486th "Tony" to call Brooklyn home. In some way he has influenced—good or bad, but mostly good—darn near every person he's ever come across. He has accomplished some amazing feats in life, including the acquisition of many traffic violations, and he's nowhere near finished. He is a patriarch, and his family both loves him and is often mystified by him. He sells real estate, and he doesn't take "no" for an answer.

The Man in the Garlic Tuxedo

Sometimes he doesn't take any answer because he's not listening. Also, he likes to golf.

He is a great man from humble beginnings. Those humble beginnings being, specifically, taking his first, gasping breaths in the arms of a midwife, in a small Italian home, while a dead chicken lay on the floor.

Italy

Having a chicken's beak shoved into his anus would not be Tony's last brush with death.

Tony grew up pretty much poor. Maybe not poor in the way we view the term presently, with flies swirling around his head and perpetually wanting, but definitely poor in that he was not afforded many things people took for granted even back then. His father was a modest fisherman. In fact, his dad was out fishing nearby when Tony was born. The announcement of his son's birth reached him via someone—let's assume it was Rosina—yelling to him from ashore, "You have a son! It was a close one though!" His response was "Awesome! I am fishing!" These are loose translations.

When he was three years old in 1950, Tony caught pneumonia. This was bad news for a young boy with no access to modern medicine, and his health deteriorated by the day. His desperate mother was finally able to locate a local doctor to come by to diagnose and hopefully help her son. The doctor arrived on a bicycle.[1] After looking at the young boy, the doctor regretfully informed the mother that the boy would not survive without penicillin. The doctor neither had access to nor knew of anyone with access to penicillin. He assured the family, however, that he had some band-aids, just in case.

I can't say I exactly understand how things work in Italian culture. From my minimal experience, I have determined the way things get done is by finding someone who might know something or who might know someone else who knows something, all of which is done very casually. Once word of mouth spread of the young boy's dire need for penicillin, someone somewhere was able to come up with it. Of course, penicillin was expensive, especially for a fisherman's family—five hundred lira, to be exact. Without batting an eye, in the interest of saving her young son, Tony's mother sold her dowry to get it.

After injecting the penicillin into—yes—his buttocks, the doctor deemed that Tony was on a twenty-four-hour health watch. If his breathing improved, the medicine had worked. If it did not, he would die. Since you are a reading a book about the man, I'll save you the theatrics. He lived. The doctor, who really didn't do much short of administering the medicine, was paid with chickens and eggs. Not as a meal—he was handed some chickens and some eggs. I am unsure how he transported them home on his bicycle.

---

[1] Tony once waited for a doctor to arrive on a bicycle to prescribe penicillin, and now he owns several iPhones and an iPad. Tony, that is. Not the doctor. The doctor is dead.

Italy

I realize we are speaking of a small, rural town in Italy and not the country as a whole, but all this talk about chickens and doctors on bicycles and dowries has reaffirmed my suspicion that Italy in the mid-twentieth century was the cultural equivalent of postrevolution America.

At seven years old bad health returned, this time in the form of Tony being generally malnourished and skinny. Nobody was quite sure what was causing this, but in Italy, appearing as though you are not being adequately fed is an unforgivable black mark on the family's reputation and grounds for talking bad about that family behind their backs.[2]

A skinny son under any circumstances should not be tolerated, but more importantly, Tony wasn't healthy. Luckily, there was a man in Siderno who passed by daily with his goats. Tony's mom, through the Italian gene of knowing everything about food, and acutely aware of the health benefits of goat's milk, would stop the guy and ask him for some milk. The man, right then and there, would squeeze milk from his goat's udders into a jar given to him by Tony's mom, and young Tony would immediately drink.

I can't even really begin to place myself into that scenario. Am I supposed to drink this? Is this FDA approved? This is the type of thing modern, middle-to-upper-class

---

[2] Many years later, Tony would witness his firstborn son return home from his first semester at college a little on the skinny side. Tony's greeting to his son, whom he hadn't seen in months, was "Joe, you look horrible. What did you do to yourself? Get in the car—we're going home to eat." That less than enthusiastic reaction is evidence of how important it is to be perceived as someone who enjoys eating frequently. I say "perceived" because it wasn't like Joe wasn't eating. Only Italian parents can manage to discourage a newfound love of daily jogging.

The Man in the Garlic Tuxedo

Americans are asked to do during survival-based reality shows.

The goat's milk worked. Tony's health, energy level, and natural body weight returned. Stories like this, common throughout the region, led to the popular Italian cartoon *Popeyo, the Italian Sailor Man,* in which the main character downs jars of goat's milk for muscles and then fights his nemesis Bruto for the rights to actual olive oil.

This also marked the beginning of a sustained period of good health. So much so that by the time he was ten, the local schoolteacher, noticing what a bright, attentive boy Tony was, asked his mom what she was feeding him.[3] The answer to that question was simple, and transcended even the benefits of goat's milk: He was sucking on fish heads.

Having a fisherman for a father meant eating a lot of fish, but not the good parts of the fish. The good parts were sold. So, for Tony it meant eating the broken parts and the heads of the fish.

Tony's mom was able to work miracles with what she was provided—soups, pastas, broken fish casserole, etc.—but no part of the fish should be wasted. Thus many meals ended with young Tony sucking on a fish head. To be more specific, as he has described it to me, he most enjoyed "sucking on the eyeballs." This is a terrible thing to imagine for someone (me) who hates eyeballs, even though the surrounding tissue (gross) has undeniable health benefits. Today, fish eyeball scientists

---

[3] I always enjoy how food remains the basis for all that is good in Italian culture. It wasn't "What are you teaching him?" or "Is he sleeping well?" or "Does he read often?" Only his diet was of relevance.

Italy

call them omega-3 fatty acids, and people buy vitamins that contain them. Back then Tony was doing it the organic way. And it wasn't just improving his health and general alertness; it was advancing his education.

His teacher would say, "Alright-a class, who-a knows-a de answer: A-two times a-two equals ... ? Mario?"

Mario had eaten bread and pasta the night prior, and is asleep at his desk.

"Mama mia!" the teacher would say. "Che scemo. Hows about ... Antonio?"

Tony, after tossing away a recently sucked-on fish head, would say, "The answer is four. NEXT QUESTION."

It wasn't just traditional school where Tony set out to impress with his omega-3-fueled energy and natural smarts. There was also, obviously, his adolescent carpentry apprenticeship.

Yes, at five years old Tony began toiling in a carpentry workshop as an apprentice. I remain uncertain whether this is a standard Italian practice or something young Tony decided to do on his own. When prodded for details, Tony's response was "Carpentry, you know ... like Jesus," as if I am totally unfamiliar with carpentry in general.[4] The point is, from five to ten years old, Tony actively practiced carpentry. *From five to ten years old.* I am thirty-five and have yet to properly assemble a piece of IKEA furniture. When I was five I was making noodle-based projects in school that my mom had to wait a few months to throw out to avoid hurting my feelings. When Tony was five he was putting additions on the house.

---

[4] To be fair, I am VERY unfamiliar with carpentry.

The Man in the Garlic Tuxedo

This experience in the trade helped make Tony the hands-on man he is today. If something is broken, he can fix it; if something needs to be installed, he can install it. That's not to say he always opts to do it himself. He is a busy man, so he will sometimes outsource small jobs, which allows him the time to stand over the person with twenty years experience in the field whom he hired to do the job and explain to him what he is doing wrong and, you know what? Why don't you just get out of the way for a second so he can show you, okay? He's been doing this since he was five.

When he was ten years old, on his graduation from carpentry school, the family moved to a new house less than a mile away. Even this short distance meant new friends and new experiences. The kids in this part of town were older, and Tony began spending a lot of time with them, seeking their knowledge. This, according to Tony, served to spark his lifelong desire to discover new things, new places, new people.

This is a crucial, integral part of understanding the man. If he doesn't know about something—rare these days—then he wants to find out. He is always seeking to be around people who know more about certain things than he does, which is an admirable quality. The frustrating part of this is when he takes some "newfound" knowledge back to his family and friends who have been trying to tell him that *exact same* thing for years. I can only imagine what it was like at the dinner table when Tony, ten, began spouting off to his family the wisdom he had gained from the neighborhood twelve-year-olds.

Italy

That said, what separates Tony from many is that he does not believe he truly knows something until he has experienced it for himself. Whatever new and exciting things he was learning about what existed beyond the invisible walls of Calabria only meant that he'd inevitably break through those walls to find out firsthand.

He already could not be contained by land. By seventeen, like his father before him, Tony had enrolled as a merchant marine. This was a program by which young men were afforded the chance to work on ships of the same name—merchant marines—which transported cargo up and down the Mediterranean Sea and beyond.

The first ship Tony worked on was the *Marco Polo*. Each voyage lasted about four months and enabled him to travel from Venice, through the Suez Canal, to East and West Africa. But it wasn't all margaritas and shuffleboard. For one thing, the cargo on the ship included mostly animals. The *Marco Polo* was much closer to Noah's Ark than Royal Caribbean. Also, Tony's job was as a busboy washing dishes. At around the same age I was living it up as a cocky American high schooler, Tony was sweating in the hot kitchen of a cargo ship, saying things like "I'll be done with these plates before we drop those camels off in Kenya."

Regardless of his social status on the ship, Tony took every opportunity to experience the world. When the *Marco Polo* docked in Africa, Tony disembarked and immediately joined a safari group that traveled to the outskirts of Nairobi, where he saw many types of animals that weren't on the ship for legal reasons—lions, cheetahs, and elephants.

While he wasn't allowed to speak to the officers and

The Man in the Garlic Tuxedo

passengers on the *Marco Polo*, he and his friends were often able to sneak in some worldly luxuries. Luxuries at the time mostly consisted of a bunch of them huddled up in some stuffed cabin, sipping drinks and listening to a band called The Beatles.

Tony's next maritime experience was on a ship called *Asia*, the sister ship to the Italian passenger liner *Africa*. By this time he had graduated from busboy to working in and around the bar, and he was able to interact with passengers who were from all over the world. The ship traveled to places like Bombay and Hong Kong. On one stop in Egypt, through a connection he had made on board, he bathed outdoors in a palace that overlooked the poverty-stricken streets. He was learning about the world, and he was living the life. Then, it all came to an abrupt stop.

When Tony turned twenty it was time for his mandatory twenty-four months of service to his country, in his case the Italian Navy. Although he was a proud merchant marine with tons of seafaring experience, he entered the navy reluctantly. The next two years would not be spent on his terms, and that in itself would be torture.

Tony was bored to death. When I first found out about his navy experience, I joked with him that I had always imagined the Italian Navy was a bunch of guys sitting on a ship smoking cigarettes and whistling at mermaids. It turns out that assessment wasn't far from the truth—only without the vessel. During his tenure of service, Tony never once stepped foot on a ship.

One of the few fascinating things that occurred during this time was when the American Navy paid a visit to the Italian base. Tony and his crewmates stood in awe of the

Italy

Americans and treated them like gods. The Americans acted the part, seniors to the Italian freshmen, with an arrogant attitude and cocky demeanor that was a welcome and strangely inspiring confirmation of the world's perception of the U.S. The crews intermingled, and this was when Tony was first introduced to baseball and whiskey, our two greatest exports.

Not long after the American naval crew left the Italian base, Tony and his crewmates received word that the Americans' submarine had been lost at sea. The Americans Tony had befriended were members of the USS *Scorpion*, a nuclear submarine that was declared lost in June 1968, along with its 99 crewmen. This came as an absolute shock to Tony, who viewed the Americans and this vessel in particular as impenetrable to defeat. The submarine itself, one of the first of its kind, was a testament to the sheer power and ingenuity of America. No one was permitted to even approach the sub at the naval base—its contents were top secret. For Tony, it might as well have been a space shuttle. As for the crewmembers, their positive attitude and spirit of adventure were intoxicating for Tony, especially amid the daily, monotonous drone of life on the Sicilian base. It seemed impossible this unbridled passion would meet tragedy head-on. This harsh early lesson on the fragility of life has remained with Tony, and is a major reason he continues to live each day to the absolute fullest, transcending the cliché.

Besides the immense sadness, the boredom also returned when the Americans departed. Tony was itching to get out of there by any means necessary, even for a short while. He discovered through a friend that a trip to the infirmary could ultimately lead to a month or two back home at no penalty to the twenty-four months of required service. Suddenly, as if by some Divine intervention, Tony's throat became sore. He went right to the infirmary.

The "doctor" looked in his mouth. It was his tonsils. Instant diagnosis. Remember, these were the days when you could knock on someone's forehead to find out if he had a brain tumor. Anyway, did he want surgery or not? There was no coddling, especially in the navy. Tony had no idea what this surgery would entail, but figuring it would earn him a trip home, he agreed.

They strapped him to what appeared to be an electric chair. They tied down his hands and feet and then tied a thick strap around his head to keep it secured to the headrest. They put a large device into his mouth to keep it open, making it impossible for him to talk. Had he been able to talk, he would have told them that it felt like his jaw was cracking in half, although I doubt they would have cared.

Suffice it to say, it's unlikely the men responsible for this surgery had any sort of license to do so. This was Italy! "I once saw my brother do this … " was all the experience required. These thoughts undoubtedly ran through Tony's mind as he watched—wide-eyed, *A Clockwork Orange*-style—one of the men grab a giant pair of pliers.

Clip, clip. Tonsils out.

They sent Tony to the upstairs hospital room, which was operated by nuns. The nuns implored him not to swallow the blood, but to spit it into the bedside blood trough. He was in so much pain, and was bleeding so profusely with no end in sight, he thought he was going to die.

When the bleeding eventually and mercifully stopped,

Italy

Tony was sent home for two months to rest and recover. Once home, he worked up the courage to look inside his mouth in the mirror, which revealed two giant, bloody scabs in the back of his throat. They might as well have been marked "The Italian Navy was here." The scabs had earned him his trip home, and Tony decided it had been worth it.

He was crestfallen to have to return to the naval base, but at least the end was near. Tony already had his sights set beyond Italy, and his encounter with the American Navy had made him more intrigued with the idea of America. As he waited at the train station to go kicking and screaming back to the base in Sicily, he noticed one of the train engineers on the platform staring intently at a small television. Tony joined him. The TV was broadcasting footage of Neil Armstrong walking on the moon.

The Italian Navy was, in many respects, the exact opposite of walking on the moon. It only stymied Tony's exploration of what was out there. He had already been making plans with a navy friend to meet somewhere when they were granted their release. They decided it should be an English-speaking country, but not necessarily England. His friend had heard that it was easy to get a visa for South Africa, and that the country was looking for immigrant workers, as long as they were white. Tony checked. He was white. South Africa it was.

When Tony left his personal prison of the navy, he immediately obtained his visa. The flight from Rome to Johannesburg in 1971 was Tony's first airborne experience. On landing, he was forced to then board a two-propeller plane to Cape Town. He shared the plane with one other gentleman—touching shoulders while sitting mere inches away from the pilot—an older fellow who made the Sign of the Cross as the dinky plane lifted perilously into the air. Tony, who is not often frightened, joined him in this gesture.

He safely made it to Cape Town, and in a *Shawshank Redemption* of a reunion, met his navy friend.

South Africa

In South Africa, Tony was able to find lodging in a rented house thanks to two brothers, Italian investors. The Bagatta brothers from Milan, of course.

One thing I have come to learn in life—Italians have an innate ability to seek each other out, no matter the geographic location. Tony could be stranded in a Peruvian rainforest, and if he happened to somehow run into a fellow member of the human species there, you can bet it would be an Italian who knows so-and-so from Brooklyn. That he was in the middle of South Africa in an attempt to leave the constraints of Italy behind and managed to thrive thanks to two Italian brothers should come as no surprise. One of the themes of Tony's life is that no matter how far he traveled from Italy, Italy followed.

Tony began working as a bartender at a five-star hotel

owned by the brothers, called the Heerengracht.[5] He was having the time of his life. Young and free, tending bar at a thirty-two-story hotel in beautiful Cape Town? It doesn't get much better. To this day, Tony's affection for South Africa remains remarkably strong. When he discovers that someone is from South Africa—and by "someone" I mean a waiter at a restaurant—he will spend most of the evening ignoring us and happily reminiscing about his time there. Also, simply being from South Africa instantly earns you Tony's complete trust, and South African waiters are the only ones besides Italian waiters to whom Tony will say, "I don't need to see the menu—bring me whatever you recommend."

As tends to happen in this stage of life, Tony fell in love. Among various interests, they shared the same birthday, which indicated to Tony this must be destiny. As also tends to happen in this stage of life, it didn't last. Tony was heartbroken and, according to him, this is when he became familiar with Glen Campbell. Yes, the country musician. A depressed Tony would sing Glen Campbell songs at the bar after his shift was over, drink in hand, pondering the travesties of unrequited love. It's uncertain how many Italian men are introduced to Glen Campbell in South Africa, but it's probably a lot.

By 1973 it seemed time for a change. Tony had experienced heartbreak and was also unsure where his life as a bartender was leading. Although his love of Cape Town remained unchanged, Tony was also becoming adversely affected by the

---

[5] The Heerengracht Hotel is still around today. You can—I doubt at the time Tony foresaw this ever becoming a possibility—"like" it on Facebook.

realities of apartheid, which he witnessed firsthand daily on his bus ride to work. For someone who valued his freedom above nearly all things, it became difficult for Tony to live in the midst of suppression and segregation and not feel as though he were complicit in the injustice.

Making matters more complicated was that Tony had fallen in love yet again, this time with a girl from England. In fact, her family remained in England, and Tony could sense her longing to return home. Possibly for that reason, possibly as a result of previous heartbreak and not wanting to lose her, possibly because he was young and unconcerned with what it really meant, and possibly because of all these things, Tony proposed marriage.[6]

Now he was engaged, and at least one aspect of his future finally seemed certain. The engagement, however, did not prevent Tony's love interest from going to England. In fact, it prompted it. She was off to her home country to visit her mother for an indefinite amount of time.[7]

Tony decided to return home as well. I mean, he might as well let his family know in person that he was engaged, albeit without the evidence. It's uncertain how long Tony lasted this time around in Calabria without going stir crazy, but if I had to guess I would say … three hours maybe? However long it was, it was long enough for him to purchase his first car, a Fiat 850, that he would drive to England to see

---

[6] Before writing this book, I did not know that Tony had been previously engaged, so we are all learning things here!

[7] Let this be a lesson to all you lovesick kids out there: It's never a good sign when the person you love wants to leave the country indefinitely.

The Man in the Garlic Tuxedo

what was up with his fiancée[8]. On the way he passed through Switzerland and France, spending time in each.

---

[8] Although Fiat 850s *could* swim by attaching a small, motorized propeller to the rear bumper, Tony opted instead to put it on a ferry to cross the English Channel.

England

The plan, as Tony saw it, was for him and his fiancée to return to South Africa, get married, and decide on their future together from there. Maybe they would settle down elsewhere. Spain? Portugal? France was beautiful, he now knew. Anywhere was okay with Tony. Staying put for the moment, however, was what suited her, he soon discovered. Having now made his way to Great Britain and been confronted with a fiancée unwilling to budge, Tony was forced to do his least favorite thing—wait.

Not one to twiddle his thumbs, Tony found employment. He signed on with Index Glass & Aluminum, a company owned by his fiancée's brothers.

There are times in life—we've all had them, and they typically occur just before God begins to reveal our true purpose—where we find ourselves in a situation that forces us to stop in our tracks. For Tony, that occurred as he was driving around England selling windows door-to-door. Completely green to sales, Tony trained himself by listening to sales tapes as he drove between houses that were miles and miles apart. How did he get here? What was he even *doing*? Then, God got all dramatic.

While driving to and from houses selling windows, Tony had a head-on collision with another vehicle during an extremely foggy evening around the bend of an English countryside. He emerged unscathed—Tony insists his lack of injuries are a miracle. He easily could have died, but the car was totaled.

Tony had been in England for eight months. He had a job he didn't care for, a woman who, increasingly it seemed, didn't care for him, and now he had no car. Never one to overstay his welcome, Tony called off the engagement and started making plans to go elsewhere.

But where? Not home, of course. That would be moving backward in life. Tony harkened back to his time on the train platform, watching Neil Armstrong on television. He thought about how much he had admired his American naval counterparts. He thought about Glen Campbell. He thought about *The Godfather*, which had recently been released. Although he certainly defied that mobster stereotype, the movie piqued Tony's curiosity even more about life in the States. He had always had a fascination with America. He *did* have some family there, an uncle in a place called Brooklyn …

That's it, he decided—he would go to America. But only for a month or two, just to see what all the fuss was about. His family in the U.S. was thrilled to hear of his plans, although they didn't get many details other than "I'm coming to visit."

England

With a tourist visa, Tony took British Airlines to Munich, and from Germany to Kennedy Airport in New York. From an airport payphone he called his uncle's house to have someone come and pick him up. Since Tony had been vague about the particulars of his trip, nobody answered because nobody was home. They were all at a wedding. Stuck at Kennedy Airport with no money, no knowledge of his surroundings, and no one else to call, Tony bided his time by calling the house repeatedly for hours on end. Eventually his aunt, who had rushed back to the house from the wedding because she had run out of diapers for her infant daughter, picked up the line.

Tony had been saved by a dirty diaper, and help was on the way.

Brooklyn

Tony arrived in America on June 29, 1974. The next day, he met the future mother of his children.

Tony's uncle took him on a leisurely drive through Brooklyn that day, and they passed young Anna's house. Anna's father was outside painting, and believe it or not, he knew Tony's uncle.[9] Tony's uncle made the introductions, and after what I imagine to be a lot of excitable yelling and hand gestures, they were invited inside for coffee. Since it is against the rules of Italian culture to refuse an invitation of any kind, they were forced to accept.

Because of the guests, Anna and her sister Liz were told to get the coffee ready, which annoyed Anna greatly. After bringing the coffee upstairs, Anna's mother introduced her to

---

[9] When Anna was recounting this story to me, I asked how her dad knew Tony's uncle, and she said, "They were paisans!" I guess that was an explanation?

Tony and mentioned he had firsthand information about Anna's fantasy destination. "This young man has been to Switzerland ... "

Having never left Brooklyn, Anna frequently allowed her imagination to roam about what the rest of the world had to offer. For whatever reason, she had settled on Switzerland as the ultimate faraway paradise. It was where she envisioned herself should she ever manage to escape the life to which she had grown so accustomed. Switzerland meant there was something out there greater than *this*. To hear that this man now sitting in her kitchen had actually been there instantly demanded Anna's full, undivided attention.

Besides that, Anna was impressed that Tony spoke English. The courtship was underway, and what a courtship it was! Not long after their first encounter, Tony called the house to acquire the work phone number of his love interest, but was given the wrong number by accident.[10] Undeterred, he managed to locate Anna by meeting her near the train station. He would arrive at the train station riding a child's bike because that was the only mode of legal transportation he could manage. He wanted to take the relationship a step further—a request that I imagine was quite whimsical coming from a grown man sitting on a small bike with a horn and tassels—but the next step after meeting someone of the opposite sex at this time in Italian-Brooklyn was marriage. Dating, at least in Anna's mother's house, was not a thing.

Tony therefore agreed to meet with Anna's parents in order to express that his intentions were pure. Anna was not

---

[10] Or was it?

invited to this meeting about her future and was relegated to having her ear cupped to the door, trying to hear the conversation. It must have gone well because Tony was granted permission to continue seeing Anna, although certainly not without chaperones.[11]

The courtship, according to Anna, went as follows: Tony would come to the house and sit on furniture covered in plastic while her mom sewed, her dad watched the Yankees on TV, and her brother Paul made himself a hoagie in the kitchen. Ah, the life of the world-traveling bachelor! This young man who had been to Switzerland was now sticking to the sofa while Paul ate salami. Enduring the mundaneness of family home life assuredly meant Tony was indeed in love.

To get an even better idea of the conservative nature of this courtship, while visiting the hall to make arrangements for their wedding day, Anna requested permission from her mom to hold Tony's hand. She was told no, but she could hold his arm instead, a counteroffer Anna refused based on principle.

Tony and Anna first kissed on their wedding day.

Like, for real.

Once engaged, Tony accompanied his young fiancée and future mother-in-law to visit some of their friends whom he had never met.

At this time in his life, Tony was bursting with the not-so-quiet confidence of a young, experienced world

---

[11] Everything you've heard about the wild, free-swinging New York 70s is a lie. Sorry.

The Man in the Garlic Tuxedo

traveler. He had shared ships with donkeys, bathed in Egypt, did a stint in the navy, fell in and out of love, and came to America on a whim. He was the most interesting man in the world and he knew it. Sure, he was newly engaged and on the verge of settling down, but that would not stop him from expanding his horizons with his knowledge of culture, politics, art, fashion, and the like. He was a refined man, or at least that's how he carried himself.

Tony had attempted to shed the cloistered traditions of Italy when he left, but those traditions had relocated to Brooklyn because most of Italy had relocated to Brooklyn. Sure enough, the friends they visited that day were fellow Italians living in Bensonhurst.

One of the friends, an older woman who was close with Tony's future mother-in-law, was kind enough to take the three of them on a tour of her house. After all, it was important for the young couple to begin thinking about what type of place they'd like to live in once they were officially married. She showed them each room, eventually getting to the master bedroom. Once there, she pointed to the crucifix above the bed and said something along the lines of "And there, of course, is the crucifix, which you two will have above *your* bed soon enough."

Now, there are too many Italian-Catholic traditions to count, and many Italian-Catholic *superstitions* are disguised as traditions. Never put shoes on the table; walk out the same door you came in through; wear red underwear when you're going to see a jealous person and also on New Year's Eve; don't kill moths in the house because they're really St. Anthony watching over you; never verbalize when things are going well or else they'll take a turn for the worse; etc.[12] There is a fine line between superstition and tradition, but those that fall on the latter side are nonnegotiable. Among the nonnegotiable Italian-Catholic traditions is this: There will be a crucifix above the bed. That's it, end of story.

When the woman said, "You will have a crucifix above your bed soon enough," it was the equivalent of her pointing to the kitchen sink and saying, "There is where you will wash your dishes one day." It didn't even really have to be said, but it's important to talk when you're giving a tour. Tony, however, adamantly disagreed with the premise.

"No!" he said emphatically. "*That* is where I am going to put a picture of a nude woman."

The gasps of the three Italian women could be heard throughout the metropolitan area. Birds flew away and cars screeched to a halt in the street. Tony's mother-in-law immediately muttered prayers to herself while making the Sign of the Cross. Anna looked at him in horror. The friend excused herself for a moment, presumably so that she could run down the street and attend a quick Mass.

It was a demand for nude art for nude art's sake. It wasn't like Tony said, "No! I will place a Renior there." It was more like "During my travels I have acquired the knowledge that nude art is very much in vogue. Therefore, I decree there will be boobies above our bed!"

There is a fascinating dynamic within old-school Italian culture where the female must show the male proper respect,

---

[12] I have found out about most Italian-Catholic superstitions by unknowingly breaking them. For example, that time I killed St. Anthony.

especially in public, regardless of what that male has just said or done. Therefore, Tony's mother-in-law managed to play things close to the vest and chose not to argue with her future son-in-law in another woman's home. She simply let him have his say, deciding she would face this travesty head-on in the very near future.

The day following this dramatic demand for nudity, Anna's mother pulled her aside and questioned the motives of her husband-to-be.

"Anna," she said, "are you sure this is the right man to marry? Who could ever imagine such a thing? No daughter of mine is sleeping below a naked woman!"

More specifically, she questioned outright whether or not Tony was, of all things, a communist.

I'm not certain that the stereotype of the average communist includes his desire to hang nude pictures above his bed, but it's important to remember that this was all happening during the Cold War. To display a lack of allegiance to anything, be it country, faith, tradition, certain foods, paintings of clothed women, etc., invited implications of communism. Whatever Tony's ideologies were at the time, this particular demand was simply unacceptable.

Something must be done.

Drastic times called for drastic measures. Somehow, Tony's future mother-in-law managed to contact his biological mother in Italy to explain what had transpired. It led to the famous "gasp heard round the world" that children have read about in their school textbooks ever since. Once Tony's mother recuperated—I imagine her slouched in a chair, nearly passed out while barely hanging on to the telephone, with Tony's sisters and brother fanning her and giving her water—she ended the conversation defiant.

"Oh yeah? I'll fix HIM!" she assured Anna's mother, in Italian of course.

On their wedding day, Tony's mother was first in line to give the newly married couple their gift. It was a strategic move.

"Why don't you open it now, in front of me?" she asked/demanded. "Like right now."

The sheer size of the box indicated this was not a monetary gift. Tony and his young bride happily opened the box, revealing a custom, Italian-made set of wooden rosary beads that were positively *enormous*. Not even a giant could actually say the rosary on this set of rosary beads; they were obviously for display. At the end of the beads was the Cross—standard, of course—except this Cross actually featured Christ. It was like the Cross one sees in church behind the altar, and almost the same size. The gift came with the not-so-subtle verbal instructions from Tony's mother: "These would go perfect above your bed."

Above their bed the rosary went and remains hanging in their bedroom to this very day.

The rosary itself represents many things—Marian devotion, Christ's ultimate sacrifice, a devout prayer life, to name a few. Above Tony and Anna's bed, the rosary also represents the only recorded time Tony surrendered.

The Cold War was over.

The Man in the Garlic Tuxedo

[Photo of Tony standing next to a dresser, with a large rosary on the wall behind him. Annotations:]
- Installed by six Italian Catholic subcontractors
- Palm Sunday palm, standard (old palms must be burned reverently in fire, FYI)
- Standard size rosary beads as specified in Beatitudes

Throughout his young life Tony had worked as a busboy, painter, bartender, licorice plant chopper[13], gas attendant, and

---

[13] Twizzlers don't just grow like that. People like Tony work very hard to harvest them.

elevator mechanic. He was unofficially trained as a carpenter. The only sales experience he had was as a window salesman in England.

After Tony met Anna he found work bartending at a local nightclub. His cousin was in a band that played at the club and was able to give Tony a ride to work each night, which was good since the club was too far for Tony to get to on the wheels of a child-size bicycle. This worked great for a while, but then the band's gigs began getting scheduled later and later, although Tony's shift times remained the same. Relying on his cousin to drive him there was making Tony consistently late for work, and eventually he was fired.

Before that, however, Tony had been doing so well at the job that he was earning Saturday shifts. It was during these shifts that he would serve businessmen types as opposed to young club-goers. On one such occasion, a business professional out for a post-meeting drink took notice of Tony's positive demeanor and workmanlike attitude behind the bar.

The patron said to Tony, "I can tell you are too good for this job," and handed him some information about a real estate opportunity in Little Neck, Long Island.[14] Tony had initially brushed the idea under the rug, but now that he was out of work...

Tony made contact but was told he'd be unable to attend the meetings until he reviewed the required reading materials and passed a real estate exam. Basically, he needed a real estate license.

So he got one.

---

[14] To this day Tony often refers to this anonymous gentleman as his guardian angel.

The Man in the Garlic Tuxedo

Tony then attended a few meetings hosted by General Development Corporation, a company that is still around today. At that time the company sold lots in Florida and, utilizing up-and-coming young real estate salespeople like Tony, marketed those lots to potential East Coast retirees.[15] Tony didn't understand how to sell something sight unseen and walked away from the opportunity.

He did, however, come across an ad in the local paper seeking a real estate sales assistant. The job was nearby, in Brooklyn, and Tony took it. The man who had placed the ad became a mentor and someone for whom Tony worked for almost a decade.

The commission on Tony's first sale was $1,800, which he immediately used to purchase Anna's wedding ring. Sales like that were, in the beginning, few and far between, and it developed his great stamina for sales rejection, the foremost attribute of any successful salesman.

Through his on-the-job training, Tony was able to pinpoint some strong real estate investment opportunities, but to move forward he needed some help. His mother-in-law, whose bank was under her mattress, fronted him some cash. Apparently, her son-in-law's willingness to take a risk on investment properties meant he was a venture capitalist and not a communist after all.

It worked. Before long, he was able to pay his mother-in-law back. He was on his feet, and then off and running. He had even earned enough money to take his wife on a nice vacation.

To Switzerland.

---

[15] As long as people keep going to Florida to die, the real estate market there will always be alive. Just kidding, Florida. Relax, sheesh.

Brooklyn

Part of Tony's newfound responsibilities included managing buildings, and his first experience as landlord occurred in 1979, renting part of a house in which he and his family also resided.

Yes, Tony was now a family man. Anna gave birth to daughter Monica[16] in 1978, son Joe in '79.

The house was in Brooklyn—Tony, Anna, Monica, and Joe lived on the first floor, with two apartments upstairs owned and operated by Tony, the aspiring real estate mogul.

In one upstairs apartment lived a woman who almost immediately began to present problems for young Tony, and who inadvertently provided a glimpse of the type of tenant he would endure for the next thirty years. She was a smoker and a drinker, noisy, and her pets frequently urinated on the floors. Worse than that, she had a reject on-again, off-again boyfriend notorious for arriving at the house drunk during all hours of the night, ringing the doorbell and waking Tony and his family. His supposed girlfriend would rarely if ever come down to meet him, meaning that the doorbell would ring repeatedly.

One cold winter night, the boyfriend's constant doorbell ringing was yet again met with no response. Instead of leaving like a normal person, he opted to start a fire to keep warm. He somehow located a garbage can that he managed to set

---

[16] Not her real name. Monica was the only family member who preferred not to have her real name used here, no doubt an extra layer of protection from paparazzi after this book is released to rave reviews. It should be mentioned, however, that the name Monica was Tony's first choice for his firstborn.

ablaze—you know, like a homeless person—right below the first floor bay window of Tony and Anna's bedroom. Tony, who had just managed to fall asleep post-doorbell-ringing, was now awoken by the sound of flickering fire and the curious light blazing through his bedroom window.

From that point forward, Tony decided he must attempt to drive the woman out of the apartment. At this very early stage in Tony's career, such a situation was touchy and would have to be undertaken via a clever system of passive aggressiveness.[17] I cannot go into detail about the nature of the actions Tony may or may not have been active in or even aware of. Hypothetically speaking, if, say … I don't know … her cat got out or something, maybe Tony didn't say anything, or maybe Tony was the one who let it out. Who really knows in these hypothetical scenarios? The point is that his actions worked well enough for the woman to complain about her landlord to her drunkard boyfriend.

It was Christmastime, and Tony's family from Italy was visiting. They were all enjoying a nice meal together in the kitchen when the doorbell rang. Anna answered the door and was met by the upstairs tenant's boyfriend, this time obviously drunk. The two-word question he posed to Anna sounded more like a threat: "Tony home?"

Anna returned to the kitchen and timidly informed her husband that it was "the boyfriend" at the door, and it looked like he wanted to fight. Before she even finished that statement, Tony's uncle jumped up from his chair and screamed in Italian, "WHO IS THIS? WHO WANTS TO FIGHT MY

---

[17] That delicateness with tenants did not last long.

Brooklyn

NEPHEW?"[18] Tony threw his napkin down, got up, and headed straight for the front door. Some family members, including his mother, tried in vain to hold him back.

He arrived at the door and confronted the boyfriend by asking, "What do you want?" The boyfriend extended his right hand, finger outstretched in Tony's face, and responded, "YOU!"

With that, Tony dramatically removed his watch.[19] Then, with bare wrists, he jumped the three marble steps separating him from his enemy and, while in midair as if part of a Japanimation sequence, cocked his hand back, landing a punch right to the nose.[20]

The two men fell to the floor, with Tony's hands now around the man's throat. The drama was heightened further by the sounds of incessant clinking—almost like gun shells—hitting the marble floor. That sound actually came from the boyfriend's waist, where he had been wearing one of those belts that hold coins.[21] Meanwhile, Anna remained in the kitchen with her mother-in-law, both terrified at what was

---

[18] Tony and Anna recounted this story to me again for this book, and in doing so Tony prefaced the scene by reminding me his family from Italy all had/have very short fuses and very bad tempers. He seemed to be distancing himself from that description of his family, which makes what happens next so interesting.

[19] The removal of the watch must indeed have been very dramatic since it is the number one thing witnesses recalled from this altercation.

[20] It should be mentioned that at this time in his life Tony was a brown belt in Taekwondo. According to him, thanks to the various drills they performed to strengthen the hands, his knuckles were "very hard."

[21] The subject of this matter came up again as Tony and Anna were retelling this story, which prompted Anna to express remorse that her husband had possibly assaulted an ice cream man. Tony assured her the guy wasn't an ice cream man, but only "maybe a hot dog guy or something."

happening. Tony's uncle was also there. He reassured them everything would be alright by grabbing a kitchen knife and telling them, "Stay here."

The altercation had now moved outdoors. The boyfriend's nose was bleeding. There was a lot of yelling and cursing in various languages. It had become a scene. It became even more of a scene when a passing car full of teenagers, noticing what appeared to be a lone, defenseless man being assaulted, pulled up in front of the house. They stopped the car in the middle of the street and got out, several of them carrying baseball bats. It was about to get all *West Side Story* without the singing.

Fortunately, one of the neighbors had called the police, and they arrived just in time. No knives or bats were utilized, and the extent of the boyfriend's injuries were his pride and a bloody nose. Nevertheless, it didn't look good for Tony's side as police approached, prompting his mother to lament loudly in Italian before falling to the ground in a heap of despair, "I'll never be able to return to this country again!"

After Tony, the obvious sober one, explained to police what had happened, he was off the hook. No charges. In fact, Brooklyn's finest doled out some advice to the young father, stating that if something like this should ever happen again, to make sure any ensuing assault takes place inside the home, where pretty much everything is legal. So that was comforting.

Two days later a moving truck arrived in front of the home. The incident had apparently convinced the upstairs tenant she should finally move. Being somewhat paranoid and wanting to know her whereabouts should any of this drama continue, Tony deftly followed the moving truck to its location in another part of Brooklyn. He recorded the new address for reference. As Tony would quickly come to learn, private investigation skills and all-out street fighting ability are just two of the requirements for any Brooklyn landlord.

With experiences such as those under his non-coin-dispenser-holding belt, Tony incorporated his own business in 1983. It was a success almost from the start. The booming economy certainly aided this success, but so too did his unrelenting work ethic. Tony's real estate business on the corner of 89th Street in Bay Ridge, Brooklyn, had recently opened when he looked outside and noticed some construction going on across the street.

Drawing upon the business savvy he had acquired over the past decade, Tony casually walked over to see if the place was possibly available for lease. He located someone who he assumed was a construction worker.

"Excuse me," Tony said, "I just noticed the work you're doing here and I was wondering—do you know if this place is going to be available for rent? I work across the street and if it is, I'd be happy to help with getting it leased."

The man on the receiving end of this question put down his tools and stood. He walked over to Tony, put his arm around him, and walked with him a few feet to the corner of the sidewalk. He motioned up to the letters the other workers were busy screwing into the façade above the front door.

"You see that name?" he asked somewhat defiantly. Tony had not noticed earlier, but in looking at it, from the letters that were installed and the ones waiting on the sidewalk to be installed, he interpreted it to read "Howe's Steakhouse." It was the same steakhouse that had been there before Tony set up his own office, and apparently it was just undergoing some renovations.

"Well THAT name," Mr. Howe continued, "is gonna be here a lot longer than THAT name!" as he pointed across the street to Tony's brand new business awning.

He had his own business now, but it was obvious Tony had a long way to go to make a name for himself on the mean streets of Brooklyn.

He was already making a name for himself in his own house, mostly "Dad." Matt was born in 1984, Anthony in '86.

Three boys and one girl, and it was becoming readily apparent to Tony and Anna that the girl was the toughest one of all. Monica shared many of her father's qualities—fiercely independent, unrelenting in her ideals, often stubborn, and a nonconformist. Much of Tony's angst during his fatherly child-rearing years was caused by his daily battles with a daughter who rejected the role of abiding, soft-spoken girl in a nuclear Italian-American family.

Anna used to pick Monica and Joe up from school on foot, bringing along youngsters Matt and Anthony. She'd go to Our Lady of Angels middle school, and they'd walk back home as a family.

Brooklyn

One day Monica, who was in fifth grade at the time, had the great idea to walk ahead of her mother and brothers ... way ahead of them. This was a huge no-no, and she knew it. She ignored her mom's yells to return and ended up crossing a busy Brooklyn street on her own. Anna was livid. To teach Monica an instant lesson, she and the boys hid behind a tree. When her daughter, confidently exercising her independence, turned around, no one was there. Predictably, she panicked. To teach Monica a long-term lesson, Anna said, "Wait till your father gets home."

There is a wonderful scene in the movie *A Christmas Story* where Ralphie gets into a fight at school, and more than anything else he fears his father's arrival home from work. When his father does arrive at the dinner table, Ralphie's mom downplays the incident, and the boy is saved. That pleasant and heartwarming scene is the opposite of what happened in this particular instance.

Anna waited until everyone began eating to reveal to her husband what had happened that day.

Tony dropped his utensils.

"YOU WHAT?"

His face turned beet red. There are unconfirmed reports of smoke coming out of his ears. His anger at having a daughter with the audacity to defy her mother and walk home by herself proved uncontainable. He was about to blow. The boys privately thanked God they had remained at their mother's side on the walk home, although there was no guarantee they would be spared here because they knew their father could spew his rage haphazardly. Their sister put on the brave face of defiance but braced for the worst. Tony clenched his eyes, raised his fists in the air, and slammed them on the table with all his might.[22]

Every dish and food item on the table became suspended in midair. The force of the blow sent shockwaves through wood and spines. The dishes deferred to gravity and crash-landed, spilling food and drink on laps and elsewhere. Anna gasped. Dinner had become a war zone, and there was blood.

When Tony's own dish landed it broke, and a piece fell off and sliced him on the side of the hand, opening a deep wound that bled profusely. If there was any possible thing in the world that could have raised his level of anger—already at "eleven"—it was this. Although his hand was throbbing, he ignored the gaping wound and stared into his daughter's eyes, and through clenched teeth he telepathically drove home the message to never try to walk home by herself ever again. She got the message, loud and clear.

He then got up and slowly walked upstairs to tend to his injury, muttering profanities and leaving behind a trail of blood droplets. Monica, as part of her punishment, was obligated to clean up the blood, and also suffered additional consequences that mostly involved a lack of television and chocolate. The lesson was clear: Walk home from school by yourself again, and you'll be on your knees cleaning your father's blood off the floor by day's end.

Monica certainly had a healthy fear of her father, but she just couldn't get out of her own way sometimes. For her,

---

[22] Italian law dictates that flipping over a table in anger is a life requirement, but banging violently on a table is also accepted as long as something is damaged.

getting in the last word always provided a greater reward than the risk of the inevitable, subsequent punishment. Sure, she argued with her dad many times, but she most often dug her holes while fighting with her mom. A poor choice of words for her mother bore a significantly greater punishment from Tony than anything she could say to him directly. During a particularly heated argument with her mom in the kitchen one day, Monica committed the cardinal sin of youth. She became so upset that she screamed the fateful words of many a forlorn adolescent: "I HATE YOU!"

From another room Tony's ears perked up like the antennae of discipline. He rushed to the kitchen. "What did you say?" he asked his daughter in a disturbingly calm manner, a preface to the storm.

"I said, 'I hate you!'" she yelled back at her mom for confirmation, then ran upstairs to her room, slamming the door behind her.

Also behind her was her father, who had charged up to her room as well.

He barged into her room where she had just fallen face-down in her bed pillow to wallow in misery. He grabbed a hold of her mattress and flipped her off of it, and she landed on the box spring. Without any care for his surroundings, he gruffly and forcefully dragged the mattress down two flights of stairs and dropped it on the floor of the family's basement.

That is where Tony's daughter slept that night. In complete darkness, on a mattress in the basement.[23] Right after dinner and without any TV. If she hated her family, she could

---

[23] In Tony's defense, the basement was finished. I'm pretty sure all Italian-American basements are finished because every room must be suitable for eating.

get a little taste of what it felt like to be separated from them during sleeping hours. Anna—the original victim of Monica's scorn—pleaded with Tony for a mere night-light for their daughter, but he refused. Again, Monica learned her lesson.

I think. To this day Monica maintains that her biggest regret from that incident was that she couldn't watch *Perfect Strangers*. She loved Balki. She is so stubborn.

Discipline, if not evident from the previous anecdotes, was an important part of Tony's house when the kids were growing up. They were raised to be polite and respectful. You didn't walk home by yourself against your mother's wishes, and you certainly didn't direct the word "hate" at a loved one. This is all understandable. There were other things, however—things for which no one was really at fault—that could set Tony's wrath in motion.

Joe was and is, in many ways, the polar opposite of his older sister. By all accounts he gave his parents no trouble whatsoever growing up, and he probably appeared to be even more low-key when set against the drama that seemed to follow Monica. Even with a laid-back demeanor at his advantage, his childhood was not bereft of his father's discipline.

The family was on a vacation in Canada. They were having dinner at a nice restaurant near their hotel one evening and everyone was in good spirits. So much so that Tony was fooling around with his nine-year-old son at the dinner table. He would try to poke him and Joe would swipe his father's hand away. This eventually turned in to some form of tickling. They were laughing and giggling, a father and son being silly and enjoying their time on vacation.

As this was all happening, Joe's tone began to change a bit. He was still laughing, but he pleaded with his dad to stop. Tony did not stop; he was having too much fun. He continued with the horseplay, but through laughter that sounded like fear, Joe kept telling him to stop. Others at the table similarly pleaded with Tony to stop. Anna said in a forceful whisper, "Tony, stop it! You're hurting him!" Monica looked on with great interest, sensing something was about to go down.

"Dad, stop it!" Joe said.

Tony kept tickling.

"NO, DADDY, NOOOOOOO!"

And with that, unable to contain it any longer, Joe let out a fart that sounded like a steam engine ship blowing its horn.

Tony finally stopped.

It seemed like everyone eating at the restaurant dropped forks at the same time. The record scratched. All eyes were on their table.

Tony's face grew red with embarrassment, which turned to anger. Part of the reason for the anger was because his daughter was cracking up uncontrollably across the table. He was not amused. He gave Joe a sustained, stern glance of disapproval and issued his decree: Go back to the hotel room without dinner.

Anna took Joe, a victim of his involuntary gas, back to the hotel while the rest of the family ate dinner in virtual silence, except for Monica's hushed snickers. Later that evening Anna would go out and get her son something to eat, and rightfully so, considering the whole thing was Tony's fault.[24]

Life with Tony was not without its minor emotional scars. But that is the price of learning valuable lessons.

Joe never farted loudly in a crowded restaurant again.

It was a hurried life. Tony was running his own business, which meant managing buildings, dealing with tenants, selling and renting property, and overseeing an office full of varying personalities. It was not easy, and it required a lot of Tony's time. He was home late and out the door early, and the fires followed him everywhere.

He was also the father of four kids, and Tony valued immensely his role as dad and refused to allow his children to play second fiddle to his career. He was an active part of his kids' lives and took full advantage of his time at home, however minimal. But time at home also included addressing any issues with the home itself. He was father, husband, realtor, mortgage broker, landlord, backyard soccer coach, plumber, and electrician, among many, many other things. Oh, and student. During this time Tony had returned to school to earn his GED.

---

[24] When Monica first told me this story, after I finished laughing hysterically for about twenty minutes, I felt such deep sympathy for Joe. I figured the next time I saw him I would run up to him and say, "Joe, I heard the fart story. I am truly sorry. C'mere, buddy," and give him a bear hug. Then while we were hugging I would say repeatedly, "It's not your fault!" like Robin Williams says to Matt Damon in *Good Will Hunting*. I never did that because I couldn't stop laughing, so it would have seemed disingenuous. But still.

Brooklyn

It was a restless existence, and Tony didn't rest. There was little time for sleep. He did, however, occasionally crash.

It was an early Saturday afternoon in the late 1980s, and Tony, after a long morning of doing who knows what, had involuntarily fallen hard asleep on the couch. There was an intercom in the family's old Brooklyn home that synced to a stereo (only the latest technology for Tony). One of the kids—to this day no one will say who was responsible—had turned the intercom to max volume, which was something for which they had frequently gotten in trouble. Anna innocently turned on the intercom to listen to music as she did chores throughout the house. The sudden, blaring music violently awoke Tony.

Startled and frightened, he assumed the worst—not that a popular musical act had invaded his family's home, but that the hot water heater in the basement had burst.

He jumped up and screamed, "HOT WATER HEATER ... BURST ... EVERYBODY OUT OF THE HOUSE!"

The confused family was slow to evacuate, mostly because they were howling with laughter, which frustrated our hero. Obviously, Tony had fallen asleep not by counting sheep, but by counting his mounting concerns about the family's hot water heater. To this day, whenever he hears Rick Astley, he gets the unmistakable notion that somewhere a hot water heater is about to blow.[25]

---

[25] In an episode of more recent vintage, Tony, sound asleep on the couch, awoke suddenly and screamed at his wife, "ANNA, GO TO SAFEWAY AND GET PINEAPPLES," and then fell back asleep. As a result, Tony and Anna now purchase *two* pineapples every time they go food shopping—one to eat and one for emergencies only.

Pennsylvania

Tony and his business were doing well enough that he was able to get the family a small vacation home in a popular East Coast getaway destination, the Poconos in Pennsylvania.[26]

An extended stay at the Poconos house was the plan for Memorial Day weekend of '89, and Tony even promised to arrive home from work early that Friday so the family could beat the holiday traffic. In a move that surprised absolutely no one in the family—he is not exactly renowned for promptness, regardless of promises—Tony did not get home from work early.

So they got a late start, and on Route 80, before the Delaware Water Gap, they hit a cluster of traffic. Tony, however,

---

[26] Anyone who lived in the tristate metropolitan area in the 80s has the Mount Airy Lodge—a resort in the Poconos—commercial etched into their brain: "All you have to bring ... is your love of everything."

as is often the case when he is faced with obstacles caused by his own tardiness, remained undeterred. As a matter of fact, ahead was an exit, and while not many local drivers knew it at the time, the exit, if you knew how to navigate it, could lead a person past the Water Gap just the same.

The exit was still probably one hundred yards ahead, and the traffic wasn't moving at all. There was no reason to wait when he could take the shoulder, so Tony began inching his way out of the right lane in an attempt to ride the shoulder. In doing so, he was presented with another obstacle.

The small pickup truck in front of him, which contained a "Pennsylvania hillbilly,"[27] noticed what Tony was doing and began moving his truck as well so as to block him. One can assume this man thought Tony was going to ride the shoulder and merge back into a better position within the traffic, and felt it his duty to prevent such an action.[28]

This did not please Tony. He laid on the car horn, to no avail. This man was trying to intimidate Tony and have him return to his place in line. Considering his family was in the car, Tony swallowed his pride and did the only sensible and mature thing a grown man can do in this scenario: He rolled down his window, calmly informed the driver of his intentions, and asked if he could please proceed.

Just kidding. He spat on the guy's truck.

It was a brash form of vigilante street justice, and unsurprisingly, the driver on the receiving end did not take to it kindly. Tony noticed the driver's side door of the pickup truck

---

[27] If the quotes don't make it apparent, allow me: not my words.

[28] In defense of the Pennsylvania hillbilly, Tony does *exactly* that ALL THE TIME.

Pennsylvania

open, and he said to Anna, who was now fearing for her life and her children's lives, "Oh, he thinks he's gonna get cute, huh?"[29] before getting out of the car.

Tony did not rush out to immediately confront the other driver, which was a relief. Although it wasn't a relief because instead he went straight to the trunk of his car and grabbed a baseball bat.

There the children sat in the back seat of the family vehicle, watching their father wield a baseball bat in a threatening manner in the middle of Route 80, yelling profanities. In the front seat their mortified mother yelled, "Tony! No! Get back here! Jesus, Mary, and Joseph ... TONY, STOP IT!"

He did stop it. Because the man got back in his truck and moved out of the way. Tony put the bat away, came back in the car, put it in drive, and the family proceeded on their merry way in silence. Poconos or bust!

If I had to guess—and really this is just a guess, although I can somehow see it clear as day—by the time they reached the house in the Poconos, Tony had completely forgotten about everything that took place on the way there. It wouldn't surprise me in the least if this happened:

"Tony," Anna said. "That was very scary what happened back there. I think you should talk to the kids about it."

"What are you talking about?" Tony said. "*What* incident? JOE—help me turn on the water valve."

---

[29] "Getting cute" = having a negative reaction to your vehicle being spat on.

The Man in the Garlic Tuxedo

On the way to yet another Poconos family getaway the following summer, Tony was driving[30], cruising down the highway with the windows down and partaking in one of his favorite vices—smoking a cigar.

Life was good. This was the type of scenario Tony envisioned while putting in all the hard work: enjoying the fruits of his labor on the open road while inhaling the sweet, not-THAT-concerned-about-cancer-yet smoke of a Cuban stogie.

The car was silent because it was like 1990, which prevented Tony from being on his Bluetooth. The silence was broken when Matt, timidly from his spot in the back, tucked against the passenger window behind the driver's seat, said, "Uhhh, Dad? I think I'm on fire."

Tony had inadvertently tossed his cigar onto his son's lap, a curious byproduct of a cigar tossed out the window when the back window is also open. That the early 90s specialized in unattractive, cloth-based, flammable shorts for boys made the situation even more tenuous.

On realizing what had happened, Tony nearly drove off the road. Anna emitted her patented, overdramatic, sucking-in-all-the-air gasp.[31] At least in this particular instance the

---

[30] Many of Tony's greatest hits occurred while on road trips, which is why Monica has always equated him with Clark Griswold. That, and because he used to wear a fanny pack.

[31] Anna's gasps are most notable for often being completely uncalled for. Her most famous gasp occurred during another family road trip years later, during which I was present, and which caused Monica, who was driving, to veer off the road, fearing an impending accident. Anna was gasping not because she had seen a small child standing in the middle of the highway, but because she had noticed the rising gas prices displayed on a gas station board we had just passed.

gasp was not *so* overdramatic, since her son's crotch was at risk of being engulfed in flames at any moment.

Tony frantically pulled onto the shoulder, got out of the car, and headed for the back. As cars whizzed by, Tony stood on the side of the highway, patting down his young son's lap with his hand, wiping away hot cigar ashes. Nobody was harmed during the incident, which is good, as death by crotch fire on the way to the Poconos would have been a heck of way to go.[32]

It was Fourth of July, and the new family tradition was seeing the fireworks in the Poconos. And the more the merrier—Anna's sister Liz, Liz's husband Carmine, and their kids made the trip as well.

The kids were a bit older, so once Tony, Anna, Aunt Liz, and Uncle Carmine set up blankets on a small area of the grassy lawn, the giddy cousins scattered to check things out before the show started.

The show started sooner than everyone thought it would. A BOOM was heard, along with a few screams. A cherry bomb had been lit and set off in the crowd, and the ensuing explosion put the surrounding families at risk. The sound alone scared the heck out of everyone. Some troublemaking kids were the culprits, and Monica and her cousin were witnesses.

In fact, they were such close eyewitnesses that when the suspects immediately scattered in the darkening night after the

---

[32] Matt, a late bloomer, credits his lack of pubic hair at the time with saving his life.

explosion, the two girls were left standing there, appearing to be the guilty parties.

The crowd was bubbling with angst, every parent wanting to find the disgraceful rascals who put their children in harm's way. The clearing smoke of the cherry bomb revealed the girls' presence. The crowd turned its ire directly toward them after someone yelled from afar, "It was those girls! I saw it!"

Pure, unadulterated fear is how Monica described her emotions at this exact moment in her life, the mob of people closing in on her and her cousin.[33]

Tony arrived with perfect timing, sensing his daughter and niece were in great danger. When I say great danger I mean—and this is from several accounts of the incident—things were about to turn physical … for two adolescent girls. It was on the cusp of turning in to one of those headline news items I used to see on "Live at Five" as a kid in the 80s, when two meatheads having a misunderstanding at Jones Beach would turn in to an all-out riot. Tony knew he wouldn't be able to physically prevent the entire crowd from assaulting his daughter and niece, so he did the only thing he could.

He yelled at the top of his lungs, "It wasn't them! I saw it. It was HIM!" And with that Tony, arm outstretched and

---

[33] The irony is, Monica is an avid follower of rules. As independent as she is, and as much as she tested her parents in isolated incidents during her youth, I have never known someone so unlikely to pose a public threat. I mean, when I bring a couple cans of beer to our development pool, which does not permit alcohol, to drink discreetly on a Friday evening, she is on pins and needles. She thinks we will go to jail. Her unease is so profound that it's almost not even worth it to bring the beer. Almost.

Pennsylvania

finger pointing, located at random a young man far away enough for him to make the escape.

The crowd, as mobs are wont to do, did not question this accusation, and immediately directed its attention to the innocent man who was in the wrong place at the wrong time. Meanwhile, Tony hurriedly motioned for everyone to gather their things and get in the car.

They sped off. In the rearview mirror the mob continued to become unhinged. No one knows what happened to that poor man. Hopefully he made it out alive.

If you're out there, buddy, Tony would like to say, "My bad." They just wanted to see some fireworks. And they kind of did.

New Jersey

In 1993, Tony moved the family from Brooklyn to New Jersey. It was not a welcome change for everyone involved. Monica, already in high school, had friends, her home—her whole life—in Brooklyn, and went to the Garden State kicking and screaming.[34] She has never fully forgiven her father. Tony's mother-in-law, who lived nearby in Brooklyn, enabling her to see her grandchildren at will, absolutely resented the move, and often refused to visit the new house out of spite. She never fully forgave her son-in-law.[35]

Despite such division, Tony knew the move was the right

---

[34] To this day Monica adamantly resents my home state, always willing to get in a dig regarding anything from its traffic patterns, the nature of its inhabitants, to its pride in musicians like Springsteen and Bon Jovi, both of whom she also cannot stand. I know part of her has an affection for New Jersey, although I also know she will never admit this.

[35] Italians holding grudges is an unfair stereotype but OH MY GOODNESS it is true.

one for the family. At the forefront of the real estate business and increasingly becoming a borough institution himself, Tony had a unique vantage point from which to witness the Brooklyn landscape changing, and not necessarily for the better. Things were different, less neighborhood-y. The cost of living was becoming absurdly expensive, which somewhat played to Tony's advantage from a business perspective, but not from a personal one. Space was increasingly tight, people becoming more agitated. Not that he considered Bay Ridge unsafe, but it definitely wasn't trending toward *safer*.

The family needed space to roam, Tony figured. *He* needed space to roam. He had earned it. They moved to the Jersey 'burbs.

Social interactions and nostalgia aside, the only one truly inconvenienced by the move was Tony, who now had to commute into Brooklyn each and every day, paying to cross the Verrazano Bridge though wind, sleet, rain, and snow.[36] It was a worthwhile sacrifice, however, because Tony's office building on the corner of 89th Street had become a familiar sight.

It was from that office that Tony looked out the window on a regular ol' workday in the mid 90s. He noticed construction going on across the street, just as he had more than a decade earlier. This time, workers were taking down the letters that formed the name "Howe's Steakhouse." And this time it was not simply for renovations.

With a sly smirk of pride, Tony continued his work. It

---

[36] It currently costs fifteen dollars to cross the Verrazano Bridge. *Fifteen dollars*. New York is absurdist paradise, but the rate to cross the Verrazano Bridge is the most absurd thing of all.

New Jersey

turned out the original Howe—the man with whom Tony had his acrimonious encounter—had passed the business down to his kids years earlier. The Howe kids sold it, and the letters being raised now spelled "Chadwick's."

Twenty years since he'd arrived from Italy with nothing, Tony now had the most recognizable name on his corner of Brooklyn.

It was a beautiful house on a decent amount of land, in a cul-de-sac within a quiet, safe, well-to-do town. It wasn't far at all from various Jersey Shore beaches. The nice ones, not the ones from TV.

Joe was about to start high school anyway, so he shrugged, not caring his new school was in New Jersey as opposed to Brooklyn. Soon he'd discover golf, eventually imposing the glorious[37] game on his father and brothers. Jersey offered plenty of places to indulge in such an activity.

Matt and Anthony were young, and their new home easily became just that—their new home.

It was an adjustment for Anna, but she made do. A couple years after the move, Aunt Liz, Uncle Carmine, and the kids followed, moving to a house in the adjacent town, five minutes away. Anna was happy.

Monica? Holding true to her promise, the first chance she got she fled New Jersey and went right back to New York where she belonged. She enrolled at NYU in 1996. Her dorm

---

[37] It is not glorious.

building freshman year also housed my best friend from high school, whom I visited frequently from my school of choice in Baltimore.

Eventually, paths were crossed. I fell for Monica—beautiful, smart, thoughtful, funny—instantly. After our first date, I knew she was the one. After our second date, I decided to start saving for the ring. Before our third date, it was time for me to meet her dad.

What I Know

I had actually planned to ring the doorbell to Monica's parents' house when I picked her up for our second date, but as I pulled into the driveway she was already running toward my car. She said her parents were having a dinner party with a bunch of their friends, and everyone was busting her chops about going out on a date, and she didn't want to subject me to the good-natured ribbing she had just endured. Her dad especially, she said, was in rare form, and although he always meant well, he had been known to offend by accident.

This was fine with me. I was already a bit intimidated by the whole situation. A gorgeous Italian girl born and raised in Brooklyn with three younger brothers and a father direct from Italy? Yikes.

I had my perception of what meeting her brothers would be like. I feared it might involve noogies and playful yet aggressive warnings about not breaking her heart and, after it

The Man in the Garlic Tuxedo

was confirmed I would not, a demand we go to the club and get into a fight to solidify our bond.

I would soon discover this couldn't have been further from the truth. The first time I met Anthony he came downstairs covered in poison ivy medicine and said to me, in an adolescent, screechy voice, "Hey, man." Joe and Matt were totally cool. I would be fine. From her three brothers there was never any feeling they must protect her, and when things got serious I received a more sympathetic vibe, like "You sure you're cool with this, *marrying* her?"

But it's always harrowing to meet the father. Even more so in my case, because meeting Tony came with *a lot* of instructions.

I was prepped accordingly. Monica reminded me not to worry if he asks me this, and not to think it's weird if he does that—that's just him. Also, his Italian sense of humor can often be lost in translation, so just … bear with him. I'll understand someday. I think she was more nervous than I was.

And it wasn't like these instructions came with even a tinge of embarrassment, which is what I found so fascinating. It had already become apparent through the many conversations we'd had that Monica held her father in the highest possible esteem. She respected him immensely, appreciated how he had raised her and her brothers, admired beyond words everything he had accomplished, and valued his opinion above that of any other person, myself included.

Yet, the instructions. It was quite the dichotomy, and from afar it didn't seem as though I'd ever be able to grasp its nature. *Will I* understand someday? But before worrying about far off into the future, it was important that I meet the man first.

I was standing in the kitchen having already met Anna as Tony walked through the back patio door. He had just taken the family's Jack Russell Terrier, Tibby, to the backyard for what he would frequently describe as "poo-poos and pee-pees." He was wearing a huge smile, and he immediately offered me a drink he had personally made in preparation for my visit.

We sat at the kitchen table and talked. Anna wanted to know more about my father, who Monica had previously revealed was a Catholic deacon, which had already gone a long way toward their potential acceptance of me. Tony's accent was strong, but I understood every word easily, and the tone of his voice, his body language, and general demeanor put me completely as ease. By the end of our kitchen table conversation, it felt like we had been talking for hours, even though it was only about twenty minutes, and I mean that in a good way. I felt ... at home.

Armed with an invite to return soon for a nice, home-cooked Italian meal, I left with Monica for the movies. Years later I would discover that, after we walked out the front door that evening, Tony immediately turned to Anna and said, "*That* is the man she is going to marry."

Besides seeing into the future, Tony had other talents, I would come to learn.

The Chef

I would take Tony and Anna up on their meal offer, and my wonderfully developing relationship with them would be instantly sealed thanks to my obvious love for ~~their daughter~~ food.

Food, food, more food, food, and then more food, each molecule of food more delicious than the last. Would I like more food? They'd be happy to make more food; it would not be a problem.

"No, no, that's quite alright—I have plenty of food," I said. "Too much food, in fact."

Nope, they did not accept that answer. They both got up to make more food.

"Am I dead? Is this heaven?" I asked.

They laughed. Hungry *and* mildly funny? I must be a keeper.

The Man in the Garlic Tuxedo

Anna made some of the food—she is more by the recipe book. Tony made the rest—he cooks with instinct.

Indeed, Tony is a food *artiste*. He has never followed a recipe. A recipe tells you what to do, and Tony is a renegade. He cooks from inspiration, from his gut. He has never made the same dish in exactly the same way,[38] and his only prerequisite is freshness. I don't know a lot about the technicalities of food, but it didn't take me long to know that I'd take a home-cooked meal from Tony over one from any restaurant, any day.

Surely Tony and Anna were skeptical about welcoming a pale Irish boy into their close-knit, Italian fold, but once they discovered my affection for food, I might as well have been a Calabrese prince who arrived on a white donkey to marry their daughter.

It took me quite a while to understand this dynamic: So wait, let me get this straight. You're going to make a ton of delicious food, and you're going to be extremely happy about me eating all of it? You're not going to think I'm a mooch, but will instead draw immense pleasure from my ability to stuff my face? My gluttony will somehow validate all of your hard work? How is this possible? WHAT IS THE CATCH?

Tony in particular appreciated not just my love for food in general, but also my taste for fish, which the rest of the family didn't care for as much. There are also very few foods I won't at least try, so he could be more adventurous in the kitchen.

---

[38] For years I have been trying to learn how he makes pesto, but every time he tries to teach me, he will swear off an ingredient that he told me to definitely use the previous time.

The Chef

I began to get the sense that many meals were made specifically for me, and no one else seemed to mind, as if it were a relief for them. Tony no longer had to pressure Joe to eat a piece of the giant fish sitting on the table—its bones exposed, its dead eyes staring through Joe's soul—because I had already finished it. Plus, nothing went to waste, which pleased Anna since she no longer had to throw perfectly good food away while making the Sign of the Cross and asking for her mother's forgiveness from heaven. Before any dish was sent to the sink, its remnants were placed into my dish. I could hardly believe my good fortune, and it seemed like Tony and Anna felt the same.

One thing Tony values immensely is conversation over meals, and my garbage disposal of a stomach would allow for those conversations to go deep into the night. This is how I got to know him, how he got to know me. We bonded in other ways—he would take me golfing with the boys, we'd go out to watch the game, he'd make me watch him fix something around the house and I'd pretend to pay attention—but we mostly bonded over food.

It was over a meal at a restaurant that I asked him if I could marry his daughter. He said yes and slapped me affectionately on the shoulder several times as he tried to refrain from getting emotional. Anna was there too, and she didn't pretend to hide her emotions. They were so happy, as was I. But more importantly, did I want to order something else? I still looked hungry. Maybe it was because I was nervous. Waiter?

The Man in the Garlic Tuxedo

Tony and Anna met my parents the day Monica and I were engaged. This was more of an exchange of pleasantries, however, because so many people were around that day that our respective parents were deprived of one-on-one time. As a side note, that day very much resembled the scene where the parents meet in *My Big Fat Greek Wedding*, the only difference being that alcohol does not adversely affect my dad, and my mom doesn't bake.

The first time they truly met was when the six of us made a trip to the famous Gargiulo's restaurant in the Coney Island section of Brooklyn, where Monica and I planned to have our wedding reception. Tony would not be cooking, but his palette would be the ultimate judge of whether or not this was a worthy location to celebrate marriage. He had dined at Gargiulo's many times, and I'm pretty sure his mind was already made up. Nevertheless, it was crucial that we discuss the food at our wedding over food.

This dinner was a very stressful thing for me. Not only were my parents going to be spending quality time with my future in-laws in my presence, but we also were going into Brooklyn.

Going to a place like Brooklyn, or the city, or anywhere outside of the East/New Brunswick, New Jersey, area is, for my parents, like being on an episode of *The Amazing Race*. There are questions like "How are we going to park?" and "Jude, did you print out the directions?" and statements like "We should leave eight hours beforehand to beat the traffic," and "I don't know where you think we're going to park at that time of day!" and "What tunnel does the paper SAY we should take?"

The Chef

In that respect alone, the difference between Tony and my parents is stark. Tony will drive into Brooklyn on a whim on a Sunday afternoon to pick up a piece of sea bass from the Chinese market; my parents plan six months ahead of time if one or both of them has to go to Newark Airport, and they still usually recruit someone else to drive. I figured the only way to circumvent this part of the stress was for me to drive.

I drove Anna's car because it fit us all. As it turned out, we were going to pick up Tony from work and then go to the restaurant. This was assuredly going to be Tony in his element, and my parents would be witnesses to the lion in the jungle. Unfortunately, the stress had now transferred to Anna.

Picking her husband up at work made sense logistically, but experience had taught her to be wary. If he had a bad day at work, there was no telling what he would say or do in the immediate aftermath. More importantly, she knew there was no way in heck he was going to be ready.

Tony was not ready. It was rush hour in Brooklyn. We had reservations. He recommended we double-park in front of his office while we waited. All I can say is thank God I was driving and not my parents, and especially not Monica. She is an anxiety attack waiting to happen when parking in an area where parking is not permitted. She won't do it. She couldn't wait near the curb in the arrivals lane of an airport if her life depended on it. She'll drive away the second she believes someone of authority is approaching the vehicle, even if that someone is a small, lost child. Though not as extreme, I am sympathetic to her plight, which is why it's always a joy when Tony recommends doing what *he* would do in a situation: "Just double-park," or "Tell them you want a discount of

The Man in the Garlic Tuxedo

seventy-five percent," or "Don't worry about what's on the menu—ask them what they *really* have."

So I double-parked, and we waited, and waited. Anna was a ball of stress, hands in the air, checking her watch, apologizing to my parents. My parents were fine though. That's the thing about my parents, and it's a trait I most certainly share—if people are waiting for them, the tension between them will explode in a flurry of raised voices and condescending remarks. If they are waiting for someone else, they're totally cool. Tony is the exact opposite of that.

As we waited, someone pulled up next to us, stopped, and then the driver got out of the car and ran across the street. Triple-park! Man, I love Brooklyn. I thought Anna was going to pass out. It was then that Tony finally emerged from the office. He indicated he was going to drive, which was fine by me. I hopped out and joined my parents in the back. Tony hopped in, threw his briefcase and papers at Anna and joyously welcomed my parents to Brooklyn.

"Jack, Judy! So happy to see you! Ready for some good food and ... *(cell phone rings, looks down)* What the fff ... *(picks up)* Hello? What? I told you already, fifth floor. Apartment 5C. Bring a wrench ... *(hangs up)* So happy to see you guys!"

The only problem was, we were stuck. My guess in that moment was that Tony was going to lay on the horn until the person who had triple-parked reemerged. I was wrong. He put the car in reverse. He was going for it.

A person riding a skateboard could not fit through the space we had, much less an SUV. Tony yelled, "Jack, how'm I looking back there?" to which my dad replied,

The Chef

diplomatically, "Umm, not sure we've got enough room here, Tony." Keep in mind that this was the second time my dad had met his son's future father-in-law, and he was already being forced to say to him, essentially, "I do not agree with this decision you are about to make." It was a nice touch though for my dad to say "we've," as if trying to drive out of this situation was a collective decision.

Tony was undeterred. He cut the wheel hard, checking his mirrors. Anna began yelling at him that there's no way we can make it. Rush hour car horns were beeping in the distance. The chaos of the situation and everyone's general opposition to this attempt only strengthened Tony's resolve. Insurance information was about to be exchanged.

Thankfully, in the nick of time, the triple-parker got back into his vehicle and rejoined the traffic flow. We all breathed a sigh of relief. Tony viewed it as only a minor convenience. He definitely would have made it, he assured us.

My dad was cracking up, and so was my mom. They had officially met Tony, and they really liked him.

Oh, and we had a great time at dinner. My dad had an allergic reaction to the shellfish. Tony made sure to alert him as to how swollen his face looked.

Never is Tony's cooking prowess more on display than during the holidays, specifically Christmas Eve and New Year's Eve. On those days, Tony and Anna invite every single family member (including boyfriends/girlfriends/boyfriends' or girlfriends' parents/college friends/work acquaintances[39]/ drifters) to their house for a massive feast. How massive is the feast? It lasts—this is not a joke—approximately seven hours and has—this is also not a joke—an *intermission*.[40]

Tony cooks for everyone, and the process begins days, sometimes weeks, in advance. The Italian Christmas Eve tradition is called "The Feast of the Seven Fishes," although, according to Wikipedia, "families have been known to celebrate with nine, eleven, or thirteen different seafood dishes." Guess which family celebrates with thirteen different seafood dishes? Let me start over.

The Italian Christmas Eve tradition is called "The Feast of the Thirteen Fishes." According to Wikipedia, "the celebration commemorates the wait, the Vigilia di Natale, for the midnight birth of the baby Jesus," like when Mary and Joseph, in the famous Bible story, dined on thirteen different fish dishes in the stable while waiting for Jesus to be born. I am not sure that is accurate, but I do not ask questions when it comes to food.

Tony cooks them all—clams, crab legs, lobster, oysters, octopus salad (my fave), filet, calamari ... oh, and also stockfish. Not to be confused with fish stock, stockfish (Tony and Anna and other Italians pronounce it like "stalk") is a white codfish that must endure a method of preparation that involves leaving it soaking in water for weeks. This process unfortunately produces a putrid smell that travels for miles and

---

[39] If an Italian coworker asks where you're spending the holidays, you are spending the holidays at that person's house, regardless of your answer.
[40] Food is served during intermission, but it's light fare.

The Chef

can penetrate all barriers. Tony soaks the stock in the garage for weeks, and everyone who lives in the house and also in the neighborhood and also in the township must endure the smell until Christmas Eve.

One year not long ago, Anna opened the door to the garage from the kitchen and was greeted by an Alaskan Husky, which barged into the kitchen holding a piece of stockfish in its mouth, almost giving Anna a heart attack. Apparently, the garage door had been left open and a local canine, seduced by the overpowering smell of stockfish, made its way into the garage to enjoy The Feast of One Smelly Fish. Anna's screams alerted Tony, who ran downstairs and grabbed a broomstick, eventually chasing the dog out of the house, but not after some comical laps around the kitchen table. This, of course, is reminiscent of the previously referenced movie, *A Christmas Story*, when the Bumpuses' dogs invade the Parker home Christmas morning and steal the turkey, forcing the family to dine out. The only difference in Tony's case was that there were at least a dozen other fishes for him to rely on and no one eats the stockfish anyway.

That's right, everyone hates the stockfish. The terrible smell plus the risk of canine invasion are things endured in vain since there is no payoff or enjoyment for anyone. Most of the family had been turned off by the stench weeks earlier and refused to eat on principle, and those who do eat the stock will comment that it's good but they "don't really like the taste." I am not even sure Tony himself enjoys the stockfish, yet the tradition lives on. To tradition!

Stockfish aside, everything else Tony makes is absurdly delicious. And there's SO MUCH of it. New Year's Eve is no different. I mean, I literally cannot tell the difference between the Christmas Eve feast and the New Year's Eve feast. I think the concept of the thirteen fishes is just rolled over with minor tweaks—instead of raw clams, for example, we'll have clams casino. Again, the sheer amount of food involved is borderline homicidal.

I remember the first time my parents were invited for New Year's Eve.[41] I had to prep my dad on the way to the house.

"Dad," I said, "honestly, you need to pace yourself. It's a marathon not a sprint, okay? We're going to be sitting down and eating for what seems like days. There is a ton of food and there will be a genuine sense of disappointment if you don't at least try all of it. Seriously, they will comment after you leave like, 'Jack is so nice, but I don't understand why he didn't try the calamari steak.' Dad, THIS IS NOT A DRILL."

The first course was pasta with fish sauce, and from across the room I could tell my dad was eating too much. "He's going to fill up on pasta!" I whispered to Monica. Sure enough, he put his fork down after finishing his bowl and said, "Tony, everything was wonderful," and the way he said it, I could tell he thought he was done.

---

[41] Eventually my entire family had made the holiday feast guest list, including my older sister Kelly, who has celiac disease, and her family. That meant Tony and Anna began cooking an entirely separate gluten-free meal like it was no big deal whatsoever. "The Feast of the Thirteen Fishes for Jesus, and Also Some Gluten-Free Pasta for … St. Celiac or Whatever" was what it was called, maybe. Also, one year the NYE party was pajama themed, and I looked across the big table and my Uncle Mike was there in his PJs. I was like, "Uncle Mike, how did *you* get here?" He said, "Tony and Anna invited me!" I said, "Cool!"

The Chef

"Everything?" What is he talking about? We are just getting started!

He didn't even make it to intermission, waving the white napkin in surrender.

Afterward I said, "Dad, what happened?" and it turned out he thought all the stuff set out on the table beforehand—the antipasto, cheese, olives, bread, fruit, nuts, vegetables, etc.—was part of the whole deal.

"Dad," I said while shaking my head in disappointment, "that stuff is around the house ALL THE TIME. There is a bowl of pistachios next to the downstairs toilet."

With time to prepare the kinds of meals he cooks during the holidays or on any given Sunday, Tony is a master. But, in my opinion, his true genius surfaces when he has little time to prepare and seemingly nothing to prepare with.

Tony will often spontaneously decide he is going to cook without a trip to the store, using only what is in the fridge. It's a challenge to him, and he is always up for it. He is the MacGyver of the kitchen. He can turn a half-eaten apple and a stick of butter into fettuccine alfredo with salad on the side.

For years I've had the idea of a premise for a reality show called "Tony's Kitchen," where he just shows up to the homes of unsuspecting families and cooks them a meal based solely on items already in their refrigerators. I would also appear on the show in order to translate everything and also to keep the confused family the hell away from the kitchen as all of this is happening.

The Man in the Garlic Tuxedo

Because you don't mess with Tony when he is cooking. This is why I always feel for Anna when they are in the kitchen together. She is forced to mess with him as he yells things like "Get me this!" "Get me that!" "Get over here!" "Get outta the way!" "What did I tell you about stirring it like that?" "Where is the whatchamacallit thingee?" "Why do you hide things?"

Besides addressing all of these matters while also assisting in the actual cooking, Anna is responsible for cleaning up the trail of wreckage he leaves behind as he goes. Tony will use every dish, pot, pan, and utensil at his disposal while cooking, and the splatter alone could feed a family of three. When he is done cooking, olive oil drips from the ceiling onto the stove, which is already covered in olive oil.

On such occasions, by the time we all sit down to eat, Tony and Anna are barely speaking to one another (that animosity dies quickly). For someone who prides himself on multitasking, Tony is uber-focused in the kitchen, and it's typically the worst time to approach him about anything. Although Anna is the most common victim, many have borne the wrath of Tony in the kitchen, including me. It was the only time I can recall him becoming visibly upset with me.

It was a summer Sunday afternoon at Tony and Anna's house, and we were getting ready to eat outside on the back deck. Tony was cooking pasta, and he was in a sour mood for whatever reason. He solicited my help.

It is not uncommon for Tony to ask for help from someone other than his wife while cooking, but because he is in control of all major components, it is usually just a gesture to make you feel part of the process. The help he requires is largely unnecessary. He'll say, "Mike, can you give me a hand with this? Can you just, uh … stand here and make sure the

The Chef

top doesn't fall off that pot?" Sometimes he will call you over under the guise of needing help, but he really just wants you to look at what he is cooking and also to smell it and tell him how good it smells. The most physical job I have been given by him in the kitchen—and it's kind of become my thing—is opening the wine. I don't want to brag, but I've only broken the cork in half or dropped the cork into the wine like, four or five times, at most. Maybe six.

Anyway, my job on this day was to hold the scula pasta (pronounced "skoo-la-BAAST," and a.k.a. "strainer") over the sink while he poured the pasta into it. I felt like a *man* holding the big strainer with both hands, the steam of the hot pasta in my face, not dropping one noodle as I helped my future father-in-law. He left me for a moment to return the pot to the stove, and that is when I made my mistake.

Growing up, I remember my mom rinsing the pasta with water after straining. I had witnessed other families do this as well, just as I had witnessed other families not do this. Even the Italian families I knew growing up seemed to be split on the issue, sort of like whether to call sauce "sauce" or "gravy."[42] Now, I knew Tony didn't rinse his pasta. I *knew* this. But something—maybe it was the euphoria of helping out and wanting to do more—came over me. I didn't want to overstep my bounds, so I figured I'd first ask him, "Do you want me to rinse this off a bit?" Only I had already begun the rinsing as I was asking, like someone who knocks on a door as they open it.

I don't even think I got the entire question out before Tony lunged from across the kitchen, screaming, "Nooooo!" and then slammed my hand down on the faucet lever.

---

[42] It is sauce.

The Man in the Garlic Tuxedo

"WHY did you—" He stopped himself. I firmly believe that if I were his actual son, or at least had been in the family longer, I would have endured a loud and angry diatribe, featuring many expletives, detailing my wrongdoing. As it was, the pained expression on his face—eyes clenched shut, head toward the heavens, holding back every bit of angst that was waiting to explode—said it all. Sheer, absolute disappointment. What I had done could never be undone. From the looks of things, I had ruined dinner. I lowered my head and walked slowly outside to inform the rest of the family.

"The pasta has been rinsed. Everybody please leave."

Tony grabbed the strainer from the sink and tried to make the best of a terrible situation.

Before he made it outside, I whispered to Monica what had happened.

"You did *what*? Why did you—oh boy."

She was no help.[43]

I turned to Anna, seeking solace.

"Don't worry, Mike. He'll get over it. He's in one of his moods. Trust me, I know."

Tony walked outside carrying the gigantic bowl of pasta and never mentioned what had transpired. I'm certain he could taste the lukewarm tap water on his rotini—his palette is a complex radar detector of taste—but he endured it, bravely.

I was never asked to hold the skoo-la-BAAST again.

---

[43] I asked Monica to fact-check this book for accuracy. When she arrived at this part, she didn't laugh or feel any sort of nostalgic sympathy for me. Instead, she gasped as she read it and then said, "I still can't believe you did that."

The Communicator

Tony's unconsciously brutal honesty acts as both his best and worst quality, depending on the circumstance. On one hand, it allows you to always know where you stand with him. It is a major part of the reason we as a family consistently approach him for advice—he will never mislead you. Well, that is, if you are family or a close friend. If you are someone else, and especially if a transaction is taking place, he will almost always mislead you—with great success.

With regard to the "on the other hand" part of this, we have frequently likened him to Kramer from *Seinfeld*. There is a classic scene from that show where Elaine's friend has an outdated hairstyle, but they all feel too uncomfortable to suggest that she change it. They opt to simply have Kramer meet her, knowing he will bring it up on his own. *That* is Tony.

My sister Jill can be sensitive, and this dates back to childhood. If she did something unfortunate like spill her drink at the dinner table, it was more important that my mom tend to her reaction to this event than the event itself.[44] It drove me crazy as a kid knowing that if she burned the house down, her subsequent tears would earn her instant forgiveness. A poor choice of words in the heat of one of our frequent brother-sister battles—"Oh yeah? Well your toes are gangly!"—could leave her out of commission for weeks.

Fast-forward to many years later, and my sister and her gangly toes are dating Monica's brother, Joe. Certainly the fact that our nearest siblings were dating—Joe and Jill are now married—brought me and Monica and our respective families even closer together, and the same holds true for the relationship between my sister and me. We are bonded not only by blood and experiences, but also the shared reality of having the most intriguing father-in-law on planet Earth.

My sister hadn't been dating Joe for more than a few months when she became sick with a bad cold. Nevertheless, we all found ourselves at Tony and Anna's house one weekend morning. My sister ventured into the kitchen to get herself some water. Her future father-in-law was at the kitchen counter slicing fruit. On looking at her, Tony took a noticeable step back and then made the following unsolicited comment: "Oh boy, Jill. It looks like the sickness has really spread to your face."

Jill, undoubtedly already self-conscious about the redness and sporadic acne her illness had caused, immediately welled

---

[44] My mom's intervention was necessary because spilled beverages at the dinner table caused a dramatic reaction in my dad that propelled him from his chair as if he had just been bitten by an invisible dog.

The Communicator

up with tears and then ran upstairs, covering her face. Tony remained in the kitchen, arms outstretched, utterly confused by the result of his words.

"What happened?" he asked no one in particular. "I just told her that the sickness went to her face ... "

My future brother-in-law Joe just stood there shaking his head, staring down the barrel of many more years of similar incidents.

Tony does not have a filter. With regard to this particular instance, the information about Jill's face traveled from his eyes to his brain, and nothing else in his brain said, "Sure, her face is red and blotchy, but maybe don't say anything because, ya' know, she probably already knows this, with the advent of mirrors and what not, and it probably won't make her feel that great, and there's nothing she can do about it, and also, what's the point?"

No. He sees it, he says it. Many people have claimed to call it as they see it, but few can claim to do so as often, especially when saying it is of no necessity to anyone involved.

Besides offering spontaneous, occasionally insulting commentary, Tony also frequently enjoys giving speeches. These too, however, are often spontaneous and unsolicited. He typically only has a general idea of what he wants to say and figures the speech will take care of itself on the fly. More often than not, it does not. However, when he comes to a speech prepared? Well in *that* case ... it's even more confusing.

When everyone sat down to eat at our wedding, Tony got

The Man in the Garlic Tuxedo

up and brought my obviously reluctant mother-in-law to the front of the reception hall. He then grabbed the microphone and said, "Just going to grab this phone here ... I'm not going to be long." Both of these statements were inaccurate.

He continued: "My family from Italy is here tonight, and there is ... a traditional thing, Italian tradition, with a telegram ... " As he was speaking he would sporadically move the microphone too far from his face, so only some of the words were audible. The words that were audible to those sitting nearby had yet to make sense.

Telegram? This was a foreshadowing of a prearranged presentation that involved two of Tony's sisters. That would be later in this speech that wouldn't be too long. There were things to get to before that, namely the formal acknowledgment of my mother-in-law's gynecologist.

"There's a very special person here who was the first person to put her hands on my daughter's body ... and it is the lady doctor who delivered her. Please stand up, Elizabeth!"

I wish our wedding photographer was alert enough to snap a picture of Monica's face at this very moment because I would have captioned that picture, "LADY DOCTOR?!" With this introduction the crowd was treated to the graphic mental imagery of my wife being pulled from my mother-in-law's vagina at birth, which ... enjoy your pasta!

My mother-in-law's gynecologist did a quick, embarrassed half-stand, waved, and absorbed the lukewarm applause associated with the traditional, standard wedding reception OB/GYN introductions.

Here are some things my father-in-law said over the course of the next few minutes:

The Communicator

"I'm not going to be long, if you could please applaud at the end."

Acknowledging my grandfather, Pop, who everyone called Pop because that was his name: "We call him 'Grandpa' ... "

"And if anyone has anything to say about *that*, my attorney is here! Al, where are you?"

Then came the physical comedy portion of the evening. My father-in-law delved into a joke about trying on his tuxedo.[45] I have to admit it was pretty funny—it would have been a great introduction to be followed by some heartfelt words aaaaand end scene. Regardless, the bit ended with Tony limping around and wearing a pair of gag glasses.

Then came time for the presentation. It should be mentioned that we were ten minutes into this thing that wouldn't take long. Tony called his sister, who was there from Italy, to join him up front. She arrived holding an absurdly large greeting card, a.k.a., I guess, "telegram." On the front of the greeting card were two cartoon frogs getting married, and all the words were written in Italian.

Tony's sister read the card in Italian into the microphone, and then Tony translated what was said to the mostly English-speaking crowd. Tony would often speak too far away from the microphone so the English part of the presentation became inaudible, and there were awkward pauses as he pondered the best way to paraphrase the translation. The room pulsed with the excitement of a crowd being read something in a different language while they were eating. It was around

---

[45] A curious case of foreshadowing for when he actually did run into tuxedo problems for Matt's wedding.

this point in the speech my wife considered crawling under the dais and reemerging for the cake cutting.

Then Tony's sister presented *him* with a smaller, normal-size card. It was impossible to tell what was happening at this point. Tony dismissed his sister back to her table ... and called his other sister to the front.

Tony's other sister arrived holding what appeared to be just a slightly larger-than-normal greeting card; however—luckily for all—it unfolded endlessly to reveal that it was even bigger than the previous card! Hooray! Surely our wedding would be best remembered for its surplus of giant foreign language cards. A reintroduction of the gynecologist would have been a welcome end to this presentation.

Here is how long this speech lasted. Our videographer recorded it, so to research for this very book, I went back and watched it with my wife. My plan was to determine how long it was by simply using the digital timer on the DVD player. After Tony's sister returned to her seat, there were several moments where it appeared he was going to wrap things up, but instead continued. Finally, the videographer just faded him out. Either our videographer was fed up, or the battery on his device ran out. For all I know, my father-in-law is still giving this speech today in a large, empty reception hall.

The Negotiator

As a negotiator, Tony is never more at home than in that fateful arena of lies, double-talk, and fine print—the car dealership.

In that respect alone, he is a valuable asset to the family. In a text to me, my brother-in-law Anthony once pondered the actual monetary value of his father as *a physical asset* (he was never able to nail down a figure). He even debated listing him as such on financial paperwork, like "I am worth more and should have a very high credit rating because I have THIS MAN at my disposal."

Never is the family at a more distinct and welcome advantage than when it's time to purchase a new motor vehicle. Also, as with his general availability and utter willingness to help any family member with anything, he is never put out to assist specifically in the car-buying process. If anything, it is his distinct pleasure to help, as the majority of his finest moments have occurred in this ruthless, Muzak-filled jungle, where he has collected on his proverbial stake the heads of many an arrogant dealer.

It is said, however, that one must be careful what one wishes for, and that is certainly relevant here. Walking into a car dealership with Tony is walking in with confidence, and when you see the vultures by the door ready to pounce on your vulnerable, warranty-ignorant flesh, there is supreme comfort in knowing that they will get their just comeuppances on this day. But it is important to know that this is not for the weak of heart because it will be brutal. So brutal, in fact, that you will find yourself at some point pained by the agonizing, merciless lengths to which Tony is going in order to get you the best deal, siding with the car dealer, just like the Russians began siding with Rocky in *Rocky IV*. Should you make the terrible mistake of saying something sympathetic to or on behalf of the other side—a good rule of thumb, I have learned, is to say absolutely nothing—you will earn yourself a glance from Tony that will penetrate the depths of your soul. You should also be prepared to leave without a car. Tony is a negotiating savant, but not a miracle worker. Besides, leaving the car dealership altogether is an excellent strategy that implies leverage. Also, if the dealer isn't going to come down to Tony's terms, 'tis better to leave in a blaze of glory than exit cordially. I'm pretty sure that motto is stitched on to one of Tony's pillows.

One of my favorite aspects of the process is the car dealer's slow realization that my father-in-law is the person he must sell. At first he thinks, "Okay, looks like the girl's father came along for the ride. No biggie." Then after a few questions, he

The Negotiator

wonders, "Who *is* this guy?" By the end, shirts have become untucked, insults have been traded, wars have been waged, and we, the actual car buyers, have become ignored, innocent bystanders to the process. We are only approached again when it's time for signatures.

During these negotiations, one of my favorite ill-advised strategies the car dealer uses is to appeal to my masculinity. They think I am a man who should make manly decisions on behalf of his subservient wife, which, pfft. At a Saturn dealership[46] years ago, while looking for a new car for Monica, Tony had just finished berating the salesman into submission, and then simply stood and left the room, leaving my wife and me alone with the dealer. This is one of Tony's strategies, by the way—random disappearance. Sometimes he will make a point and then just leave. Sometimes he'll give an indication of where he's going: "Get out of here with a 'finder's fee!' That's ridiculous. I'm going to the bathroom."

I know he has a purpose, although I'm pretty sure he sometimes leaves negotiations abruptly just so he can check the messages on his phone, inevitably leading to more private negotiations on his own behalf. Anyway, as we sat there awkwardly, the car dealer turned to me and began saying, in essence, "C'mon, buddy. This is *your* wife! Can't you guys make your own decisions here? I know she likes the car! Why don't you do what's best for her?"

I shrugged, my ego not nearly worth the amount of money we were about to save. Monica stared straight ahead in glazed terror, her lips pursed, a lifetime of her father's extreme

---

[46] Saturn is no longer around. Coincidence? Maybe.

negotiating methods embedded deep into her psyche. It seemed like hours while we waited for Tony's return, and when he reemerged he was holding a Styrofoam cup of coffee.

That is another one of his strategies—coffee. Usually the first question he will ask the dealer is if coffee is available. This has always astounded me because Tony is a man grossed out by many things, but most particularly coffee that is not fresh. If coffee is not to his liking, and that means not hot enough or fresh enough, he will send it back without remorse.[47] He has also deemed certain scenarios and locations unfit for coffee consumption. Airplanes, for example. Once on a flight back to New Jersey, I made the mistake of ingesting airplane coffee and felt its wrath in my insides on landing. Monica relayed to her dad the cause of my stomach pain, and he was incredulous that I had consumed coffee on an airplane, as if that were yet another unwritten Italian rule that I had violated. He repeatedly asked me why I drank airplane coffee, a question I answered in grunts. Then he kept telling Monica, as if I wasn't right next to her, "He really shouldn't drink airplane coffee. I don't know why he drank the airplane coffee." So, it has always remained a wonder how car dealership coffee, lukewarm from an old pot crusted with coffee stains and accompanied with *powdered cream*, has managed to pass his strict coffee test for all these years.

Tony stood there at the door of the salesman's office, casually sipping his coffee, and said, "I think I'm done with this

---

[47] Every time we go into Dunkin' Donuts—*every time*—he will get his coffee, take the lid off, sip it, make a face, and slide it back across the counter while telling the worker what it is wrong with it. Usually what is wrong with it is that it's not fresh enough, so we have to wait an extra ten minutes for them to brew a new pot.

The Negotiator

nonsense." He then motioned to us and said, "Let's go. We should go back to Toyota."[48] And with that, Monica's interest rate magically dropped, as did her monthly payment, and we all drove home in her new car.

Tony immediately requested coffee when he and I walked into the Subaru dealership. The dealer pointed us to the service department desk. It was there that Tony managed to pour himself a cup of coffee, which he began sipping very loudly before deciding that he would also like a bag of chips from the vending machine. He asked me approximately one hundred times if I'd like something, to which I repeatedly replied, "No, thank you." So he shrugged and put in his dollar, which got stuck.

When a little thing like this happens to my father-in-law, it never seems to result in a quick, smooth resolution. There was a young woman sitting at the nearby service department desk. Most people, faced with such a dilemma, would have simply approached her and said, "Excuse me, miss? Hi, yes, my dollar got stuck in the vending machine. Do you think there's any way I could get it back, or just get another dollar?" Tony has a different way of going about things.

First, while giving me the Italian signal for "Can you believe this?" which is a smirk with one hand in the air, shaking and making the sign for money, he slowly made his way over to the desk. There he sort of milled around, sipping his coffee

---

[48] We had not been to Toyota, of course.

The Man in the Garlic Tuxedo

loudly. The woman, sensing Tony had something to ask her, tried to make eye contact, but he sort of pretended he was just hanging out. Then, finally, he mumbled something to the effect of, "My dollar just ... I don't know ... vending machine? ... Not sure if you, uh ... *(loud sip).*"

Then, this:

"I'm sorry. Can I help you, sir?" the receptionist asked.

"Hi, yes," Tony said. "You are looking very pleasant and happy today!"

The receptionist flashed a nervous smile.

Tony continued, "Yeah, so I, uh ... *(loud sip)* ... put my dollar in the machine over there for the chips. I was hoping to get some chips. But I don't, uh ... I don't know where it went. Maybe you can help me? I don't know. I saw you sitting here ... "

"Okay, are you saying your dollar got lost in the vending machine?"

"Yeah, I was just looking at some chips, for a snack. I didn't really eat lunch. I don't know what happened."

"That's no problem. *(pulls out drawer)* Would you like another dollar?"

"I was just looking for some chips."

"Would you like another dollar? *This* dollar?"

"*(loud sip)* Mike! Look at this! Another dollar! I don't know what to say ... you put a smile on my face today. You can uh, put it on my tab! Ha, ha ... I was trying to get some chips. Should I put this in the machine now?"

"Yes, sure, you can put it in the machine whenever."

"Mike! I got the dollar. You see? It all works out. You want anything?"

The Negotiator

By then the dealer was ready for us. We walked over to his desk, although Tony took his time getting there. The time with which my father-in-law takes to do something is almost always indicative of a larger point he is trying to make. If, for example, my mother-in-law is rushing to get him out of the house, which is almost always the case when they are leaving to go somewhere, he will take his sweet time. This is often his way of saying, without actually saying it, "I think we can still make it on time if we leave a little later," or "Like hell I am going to be the first person to show up at this thing I don't even want to go to." There have been times when the whole family is waiting for him in the car, with the car running because church starts in three minutes, and someone has to run back into the house to find out what the heck he is doing, only to find him underneath the kitchen sink with a wrench, still in his pajamas, trying to fix a leak he thought he saw a week ago. In this particular case, the slowness with which he approached the dealer's desk screamed, "I will be dictating these negotiations."

And dictate he did. It was evident from the outset we would not be able to meet halfway on the car I wanted, but we ended up staying there for more than two hours, mostly so Tony could yell—literally yell—at the dealer. I made attempts to divert Tony from these fruitless efforts but was met only with a wave of the hand—*Don't disturb me; I'm yelling at this man.*

I would not get a new car on this day, but Tony would be darned if Subaru didn't take one on the chin as a result. Making matters worse was that Tony had recently executed an apparently cordial transaction with a Subaru dealer in

Brooklyn, so much of his time was spent trying to call Ryan at the Brooklyn dealership—leaving me alone with the now disheveled dealer—to get inside info he could throw back in the dealer's face. Ryan's unavailability was, according to Tony, the only reason I didn't drive out of there in a black Forester.

On the way home Tony kept apologizing, sincerely sorry he was unable to get the deal done. I told him his performance was better than the car. He reached into his jacket pocket, pulled out a bag of potato chips, and asked if I wanted some.

Text from Anthony to me:

> Dad answers the phone and after a second goes "If you don't know who I am then why are you calling me? Go ahead what do you want to sell me?"

Before heading into Schwartz Mazda, Anthony received the usual pep talk from his dad, which Anthony described as "Don't say anything. Don't seem interested. Don't even worry about talking. I'll do the talking."

Neil was the name of the vulture who first approached. His initial questions regarding what type of car they would like to see were met by silence from Anthony and sporadic nonsense from Tony.

The Negotiator

"So, what type of vehicle can I help you fellas look for today?" Neil said.

Anthony shrugged. Neil looked at Tony, who was talking on his cell phone. Neil looked back at Anthony.

"You ... don't know?" Neil said.

Anthony looked up to fix his stare at the ceiling. Tony got off his phone and mumbled something.

"I'm sorry," Neil said. "What was that?"

"So, uh," Tony said, "who installed the floors here? Is that marble?"

"Umm, not exactly sure," Neil said. "So, you guys looking for a two-door, four-door ... ?"

"Where's the coffee?"

Anthony refused to make eye contact with Neil and risk inviting him into a more direct conversation. Anthony's communication was limited and subtle. For example, when they located a vehicle to his liking, his acknowledgment to proceed further was a slight head nod to Tony when Neil was looking away.

Back in Neil's office, Tony did his usual thing of accepting intermittent cell phone calls and leaving the room. This would have left Anthony as a sitting duck were he not so prepared. Neil then commenced the familiar and feeble process of trying to appeal to Anthony's ego and personal wants.

"Don't you like the car?" Neil asked. "Isn't this what you wanted? Aren't the features fantastic? Is this your decision or his?"

Anthony astutely deflected these leading questions to talk about the weather—"You're right, it *is* cold!"—as he anxiously awaited his dad's triumphant return. Once Tony was back in the fold, numbers were discussed. As it turned out, Tony did not like Neil's numbers.

"What is this number?" Tony asked. "Is this *monthly*? C'mooooon, Neil. I thought we were doing business here."

It was then that Neil made a terrible mistake. He took the opportunity to remind Tony that he and his son had signed paperwork on entering his office specifying that they were prepared to do business.

Now, here is the thing about Tony. He is a warm-hearted and forgiving man. Sure, he's never met a confrontation he didn't like, but he is reasonable and excels at separating business from personal feelings. You can yell at him and you can insult him—not that I would recommend either—yet there remains the possibility of mutual respect once all is said and done. But there is one thing you should never, under any circumstances, ever do. *Never* attempt to convince Tony he agreed to something when he did not. To insinuate his signature was involved is the unforgivable sin. You would be much better off punching him in the face.

Tony understood what this paperwork meant and had no doubt signed such a document before. He knew it was simply an agreement to negotiate in good faith, but nothing more. To have Neil throw it back at him as leverage meant only one thing: Neil was done.

A fist slammed a desk—"No, Neil, it's YOU who doesn't want to negotiate!" Tony demanded a meeting with the manager. Neil's work was finished. He had failed.

The manager's name was Vinny. Honestly, I wish I could have been there. As an outsider looking in, I am fascinated by Italian versus Italian negotiations. I have come to realize that

The Negotiator

they generally result in one of two extremes: a lifelong friendship or animosity that spans generations. The acknowledgment of a mutual acquaintance or the realization that they were raised in an adjacent section of Brooklyn can easily result in a monthly dinner, where both parties will frequently and hilariously regale the story of how they came to be friends in the first place:

"Then I said, 'No, YOU get outta here!' Ha, ha, this guy ... *(raises wine glass)* Salud!"

But a choice word or hand gesture could, just the same, result in the respective families being forbidden to associate with one another for the foreseeable future, and by "foreseeable future" I mean forever.

I understand there are obnoxious people of all ethnicities and walks of life. There is no doubt about this. There is, however, something extra special about the obnoxious Italian person, especially when set against the calm, calculating Italian person. Vinny had a raspy voice that implied he had seen a cigarette or two in his day, and the casual arrogance with which he carried himself implied a self-assured sense of authority. That nonchalance can be intimidating for a meek Irishman such as myself. For Tony? Not so much.

Vinny then executed what is quite possibly my all-time favorite car dealer gimmick: He afforded Tony and Anthony the opportunity to look at his computer screen.

"Look," said Vinny as he began randomly punching numbers in, "we are making *no* commission on this deal. We are actually losing money on this car. I would never normally make this deal."

It doesn't matter if the potential car buyer is unfamiliar

with the dealership's internal software system, or that it can be manipulated, or the car buyer's inability to process the information in the instant he is permitted to view the screen before it's casually turned away ... what a deal! And what a nice dealership, to lose money on a car for no apparent reason. Tony was, however, unconvinced.

Conversation that straddled the line between loud talk and yelling ensued. Vinny, as a final gesture of goodwill, was able to locate a hidden piece of paper that detailed the previous six deals he had made. Each deal, according to the paper that was verbally interpreted by Vinny himself, netted him $10,000 in commission, $60,000 total. He then explained, as he sat back in his chair with his hands behind his head, that it didn't matter to him—he was going to be living comfortably either way.

Man, car dealers are the best. Being welcomed into their world of computer screens and hidden paperwork is a treat, indeed. We—car dealers and the select few of us regular citizens—are on the same team, bonded by the given car dealer's ability to massively screw over people who most certainly are not us. Who makes $10,000 commission on one car deal? That is absurd. By that estimation, it costs the manufacturer $30.50 to make the car; the rest is profit.

Also, this maneuver was intended to show that Vinny was not, in fact, trying to get one over on Tony and Anthony, but was more successful in establishing his indifference as to whether or not the deal actually got done. Regardless, the point was that Vinny is living well. Does he own a boat? He probably owns a boat.

Tony remained unimpressed. He was leaving. He and

The Negotiator

Anthony would be visiting other dealerships in the area to look at other cars. Vinny was incredulous.

"Wow," Vinny said. "I have to say, I have been in the car business for more than thirty years, and I have never gone this low on a deal, and I SURE AS HELL have never seen anyone walk away from something like this."

As a parting gift, Vinny assured Tony that the deal was only good on that specific day; it disappeared the minute they walked out that door. Tony and Anthony, unfazed—well, Anthony was at least a little fazed by the experience as a whole—walked out that door.

Anthony was not aware of his dad's true feelings on the vehicle until they left the dealership. It turned out the feeling was mutual that the Mazda in question was a perfect fit for Anthony, and the proposed deal was a very good one. Nevertheless, Tony was not giving them the satisfaction on that particular day, and besides, he was confident the deal would remain on the table. They visited other dealerships where similar events took place, but ultimately decided the Mazda was the one.

They returned to Schwartz Mazda the following week, and contrary to Vinny's promise-threat, the deal was still available. They met with the finance manager to go over the terms of the lease, and Tony immediately detected his accent. He was Greek, which was, apparently, great news.

This sort of thing happens all the time, usually at restaurants. Tony is an expert at detecting accents. It is truly uncanny and must be witnessed in person to fully be appreciated. The waiter will begin announcing the specials, and Tony will immediately cut him off and demand the waiter spell his last name. The waiter, confused, will oblige, and Tony will announce,

The Man in the Garlic Tuxedo

"You are from Libya." The waiter, stunned, will excitedly acknowledge as much, and the next twenty minutes involve the rest of us watching in awe as the two of them exchange stories about Libya. Having established trust, Tony then informs his new friend to have the chef bring us "whatever is fresh." Eventually the chef will come out from the back to meet Tony, and I have to call out of work next the day because we will never leave the restaurant. This is a hypothetical example and has never actually happened at least ten times.

So the guy was Greek, a culture very similar to Italian in its love of family, food, body hair, and general loudness. Not only was he Greek in descent, which is great in and of itself, but he was also *from Greece*. As Anthony put it, this was icing on the cake because—get this—Tony has been to Greece and also *speaks* Greek. Add that to the list of things Anthony did not know about his father until it actually happened. If I ever went to a car dealership with my own dad and he started speaking Greek, I would have to abandon my car search and take him to the hospital.

Anthony sat there as these two men, brought together by Anthony's affection for a particular model of Mazda, spoke Greek to each other. As it turned out, they knew some of the same people from Brooklyn. Can you believe it? I can believe it. Because of this Anthony earned, in addition to the already stellar deal arranged by his father, free oil changes on his vehicle for three years and a ten percent discount on all service for the life of the car.

Asset.

The Negotiator

If Tony is at his negotiating best at the car dealership, he is at his happy, relaxed best while at a restaurant with his family. That's not to say negotiations aren't involved there too.

For Tony, getting a table at a crowded restaurant is an art form that employs many different strategies depending on the venue. For example, many restaurants accept something called "reservations." One popular strategy that could be applied here is to make a reservation. But that is too simple and ignores the spontaneity of a Las Vegas family vacation during which we arrive at a fine Italian restaurant, just off the strip, smack dab in the middle of the dinner rush. A strategy that can be applied in this instance is to pretend a reservation was made.

So it was that we pushed and shoved our way into the crowded area near the hostess stand in the restaurant. The rest of us were safely under the impression that Tony had in fact made a reservation and had intended to come here for dinner all along. So when confusion ensued at the hostess stand, we were all as surprised and annoyed as Tony himself, blind to the fact that he was putting forth one of the greatest acting jobs in an Italian restaurant since Pacino in *The Godfather*.

Although I wasn't nearby because my sister and I went to the bar so that we could indulge our Irish stereotype, those close to him during the ruckus would later acknowledge that Tony had mysteriously lost much of his capacity for the English language during his talks with the hostess. This is part of his most oft-used strategy: confusion that is so maddening it leads to a quick resolution. Here he took it to the next level.

He had not made a reservation. He told the hostess, however, that he had. He then became visibly upset and frustrated when the flustered young woman, amid the noise of the anxious crowd and general hectic surroundings, could not locate his name on the papers she was furiously flipping through. In fact, what was your name again?

He had given her several versions of a name, all spoken in some form of broken English, Italian, and mumbling, a lethal combination to keep her off his scent. Other impatiently waiting patrons simply couldn't compete with Tony. He had morphed into Sammy Sosa at the Congressional hearings on steroids.

"I have a, uh, reservation," he said.

"Okay, what name was it under?"

"Uh, il bambino e salvato, right? Il pollo e morto."

Subsequently, all questions regarding whom he had spoken with when he had made the reservation were met mostly with words that didn't really exist, confused facial expressions, and exaggerated hand gestures.

And herein lies his genius. In her effort to connect the party size, name, and time, she began rattling off the names of some of the larger parties that had made reservations that evening. Surely, Tony agreed to the first name he heard.

"Yes, Plukowski! That's what I've been saying all along!"

Through systemized confusion, he stole someone's reservation.

I wasn't halfway through my beer when it was indicated to us from across the room that our table was ready. As we made our way through the bustling vestibule on the way to our table, passing everyone that had been waiting well before we had arrived, I overheard the hostess inform an incoming

The Negotiator

patron that the wait was "about an hour to an hour and a half." We had waited five minutes.

Tony wore a wry smile as we sat down, and when Anna questioned him about why he was acting the way he was, he casually revealed to us that he had not made a reservation in advance. It quickly set in that he had also, in fact, stolen the reservation of a more prepared family. Had we any doubts, they were dashed as we noticed that the chaos level near the hostess stand had progressed to Code Red. The feeling of remorse for cutting everyone else in line and stealing another party's table was quickly replaced with a great sense of awe for the man at the head of the table, and glasses were raised for cheers. To restaurant Darwinism! This wasn't the first time he had earned the family a table it didn't deserve, but rarely had he accomplished such a feat with a party of eight in a restaurant so packed. Yet another feather in his cap.

I have taken to wondering whether or not he has somehow gained a reputation within the restaurant industry, as if all the hosts, hostesses, greeters, and managers of various eating establishments, during their annual convention in Sioux City, Iowa, have discussed him as a topic, with PowerPoint presentations and everything, ultimately settling on a course of action best described as "Don't even bother. Just sit him down."

The reason I wonder about such possibilities results from one particular and curious instance that occurred in Williamsburg, Virginia. Tony, Joe, Anthony, and I were on a weeklong, merciless golf vacation that encompassed two rounds of golf per day. Each day, by the end of our second round, our hunger became overwhelming, and by the time

The Man in the Garlic Tuxedo

we had showered, dressed, and arrived at wherever we were going to eat, we were ready to ravish any morsel of food placed in front of us without even using our hands, like pigs in a trough.

One night after our usual two rounds, we went to an Olive Garden. Now, Olive Garden gets a lot of flak from a pop culture standpoint for being generic—an Italian restaurant for people who don't know about real Italian food. Surely there is validity to that reputation, but Tony, whose opinion on food I value greater than that of society at large, has an affinity for the place. Not a strong one—he would prefer a genuine, privately-owned-by-an-acquaintance-from-Brooklyn Italian restaurant—but a rational one. He recognizes Olive Garden for what it is, a franchise, and in that respect doesn't really find it to be so off-putting. Besides, we were in Williamsburg, Virginia, so it was Olive Garden or Chili's.

We walked in only to see a waiting area packed with people. This was absurd to us considering it was past eight p.m. How could there be a wait? We were so hungry. Luckily, we had Tony.

I have described to many people what happened next, and even as I'm typing it now, it doesn't seem true. I mean, not due to its outlandishness—it just seems like a hyperbole that serves to confirm the narrative of Tony getting what he wants. May I implore you, however, that I was not the only witness. Joe, for example, is not a man prone to exaggeration, and he can attest. Call him if you must; I will leave his phone number at the end of this book. (I will not do that.)

Tony walked up to the host to put his name in, at which point the host informed him that the wait was about twenty

The Negotiator

minutes. Tony turned around to walk away, and for a second it almost looked like he was ready to accept this outcome, two rounds of golf somehow deflating his purposefulness. But before such a thought could even formulate in our minds, he turned back to the host and said, simply and matter-of-factly with nary a hint of threat or sheepishness, "How about you make it *now*?"

To this, after looking down briefly at his waiting list, amid the intense glares of a small area of very large and hungry people, the host looked up, smiled, and replied, "Okay. Right this way."

We followed him to our booth.

Sometime in 2006, the bumbling homeowners' association of our New Jersey condo development sent a notice they were raising our monthly fee to $300.

The fee was already $240, absurd considering the amenities were three tennis courts, one of which had a net, and a pool that was open three months a year. They were also supposed to shovel and salt the walkways during the winter, which either didn't happen or happened too late. One winter morning I walked outside carrying a cooler full of beer[49] to put in my truck, and I slipped on the ice and beer went everywhere. For a second I was convinced I broke my back. Looking on and trying to contain their laughter was a truckload of

---

[49] Football Sunday, if you must know why I was getting ready to drink at ten a.m. That's a reason, right?

The Man in the Garlic Tuxedo

non-English-speaking workers who were supposed to have utilized my $240 monthly fee to salt the walkway the previous day.

This letter was not a pleasant read. But if we thought *we* were livid—and we were *livid*—we couldn't have approached Tony's level of furiousness on his discovering the fee hike. That's one thing about Tony that I was just then beginning to understand and admire: He internalizes the struggles of his children and makes them his own. It's completely organic and not for show. His kids' pain is his pain, and I think it's more painful for him. In fact, Tony had four kids in this fight, although only two of them biological. After getting married, Jill and Joe had also moved into this condo community.

The rest of the condo complex was up in arms as well, so much so that an emergency meeting was called among all residents, which would include the entire HOA board. Normally, Monica and I never go to such meetings, as we prefer taking the passive-aggressive approach of complaining about everything without being actively involved in the solution. Really though, who has time for HOA meetings? We weren't missing this one.

Neither was Tony.

Judging by his level of anger, I knew this would not be an occasion where Tony would sit by quietly and observe how things played out. We were bracing ourselves for embarrassment on two levels. One, not having any idea of what he would say or how he would act, and being near him as he does it. Two, verbally expressing that his daughter and son were residents, making it seem as though my wife and

The Negotiator

brother-in-law, almost thirty years old, had employed daddy to fight the good fight for them.

Any potential embarrassment was tempered by a) our frustration with the HOA and the fact that we didn't really care what was said, and b) Tony explicitly telling us beforehand to not acknowledge him as a relative during the meeting. On this night, he was a resident.

Alright then.

My general feeling of the community-wide resentment at the fee hike was limited, considering we did not actually know many people in the community. Walking into the meeting that night, I realized that whatever sense of resentment I had assumed was vastly underrated. The place was buzzing with animosity. As we all took our places in the back of the room, we passed nothing but angry faces. Words of frustration bounced through the air in all directions.

"Ridiculous!"

"Can you believe this?"

"Over my dead body I'm paying this!"

The only tinge of kindness expressed was when residents bonded with one another through a mutual hatred of the HOA.

At a table in the front of the room sat four or five members of the HOA board, including the president. I don't remember what they said, or how they rationalized the hike. It didn't matter, and their words just made it worse. This wasn't their meeting—it was a sounding board, and it wasn't long before they settled into their predetermined roles of sitting there and taking it.

Residents stood and spoke. They didn't raise their hands, they just started yelling, and the loudest yeller was given the floor. Some came prepared, with examples of nearby HOA fees and how they differed from ours. It was an obvious proud and shining moment for several of the retired residents, and you could just imagine the phone calls that took place the following day.

"You should have seen your father at the meeting last night. He really gave it to 'em! It did cause a spike in his blood sugar though."

The meeting, as these types of meetings usually do, often veered wildly off course.

"How can you justify $300 a month? And I've called the office three times about that car with the flat tire parked next to my house! Who stepped on my flowerbed?"

The crowd was in a frenzy, and even irrelevant topics added fuel to the fire. The HOA was disintegrating before our very eyes.

We sat there and watched the vitriol spew from the mouths of our neighbors for well over an hour. Even considering the HOA misdeeds unveiled by several of the well-prepared residents, I felt sort of bad for the board members. Not really, but kind of. The die had been cast, and it didn't seem like there was anything left to say, although the tension in the room never subsided. For a time, I even assumed my father-in-law wouldn't get his chance, or would simply decline on account of all necessary points having been made.

This was a false assumption.

Through my peripheral vision I saw him slowly rise from his chair, taking advantage of a very brief lull in the proceedings. Oh boy, I thought, it's going down. I grabbed my wife's hand and held it tight.

The Negotiator

His words—"Excuse me, but I'd just like to say something"—were not uttered with a raised voice, nor did they need to be. It was as if everyone was waiting for this moment all along, and all eyes focused on Tony.

He was holding a piece of paper, and his reading glasses were down on the bridge of his nose. To onlookers he most likely appeared a cordial fellow, an American citizen simply utilizing his right to have his voice heard. He began as such:

"I am a mortgage broker and also a resident here at, uh ..."

He struggled to remember the name of the development where he did not actually live.

" ... Pond Lakes."

Nope. Close though. Nobody noticed.

"And I just want to tell you ... Do you KNOW what this $300 means?"

At this question he shook the paper as if he had brought Exhibit A with him. Granted, the paper was probably a formal letter from one of his own tenants complaining about the cat in the adjacent apartment, but whatever.

"Your monthly fee is mandatory. MANDATORY!"

His voice was getting louder as he spoke. The crowd was hanging on his every word.

"That means this might as well be worked into the mortgage. Do you know how DIFFICULT it is now for a person here to sell his home? I couldn't sell my home here if I wanted to!"

That was mainly because he didn't have a home there. Still, the crowd was responding now, affirming everything. "Yeah! You tell 'em!" He might as well have been preaching at a mostly white Baptist church.

"With a $300 fee, you're not allowing people THEIR RIGHT, their FREEDOM to sell their home on the free market!"

With this he slammed the paper with the back of his hand, accentuating his point. I later commented to him that he was like Mussolini up there, a reference he did not appreciate.

"Well, let me tell *you* something ... "

He took off his glasses.

"YOU don't have the right!"

The crowd erupted. I am not kidding when I say that I thought they were going to carry him on their shoulders out of the room, into the street, and down to City Hall before realizing this was a private matter. Instead people patted him on his back as he, stone faced and maintaining eye contact with the board members, sat back down. His mini-speech had essentially ended the meeting in a state of chaos. There was no doubt the HOA had been overthrown—indeed it was, the near future confirmed—and that the stern words of a nonresident had helped spur the revolution.

When we exited the building that evening, people continued to pat my father-in-law on the back and approach him to shake his hand and thank him for speaking his mind. As we attempted to walk back to our condo, a woman hurriedly approached us, almost out of breath.

"Excuse me," she said, tapping Tony on the shoulder. "Hi there, so nice to meet you! Great speech, such a great speech. So, a bunch of us were talking ..."

With that she motioned to a small group, which included several of the more verbal participants in that evening's proceedings, huddled near the exit.

The Negotiator

"And it's pretty obvious this regime is done," she said. "What do you think about running for the HOA board? We think you'd be perfect."

Tony humbly responded, "Oh, that's uh, that's really very nice of you. I really appreciate that. The only thing is that, uh ... "

At this point we had approached the main road we needed to cross in order to get back home. Tony's head was on a swivel, checking to make sure no cars were coming and planning his swift escape from the conversation.

"The only thing is that, uh ... I don't really live here."

His voice trailed off with those words, as the six of us hustled across the street. Left behind on the other side was the woman, watching her once and future king fade into the darkness of the night.

The Businessman

At the time I first met Tony, he was still commuting to Brooklyn[50] for work almost every day, even some weekend days. Gone early and home late. When he was home, he could often be found on one of his phones, which were always buzzing. He would open his AOL account to reveal hundreds of yet-to-be-opened emails. It seemed nonstop, like his job was in constant demand of his time. The rest of the family would frequently tell me that this was nothing, that I had no idea how much the man used to work.

What impressed me even more than the work ethic was Tony's response to the various issues that confronted him

---

[50] Undeterred by the way he lost his bartending job many years ago, Tony *does* sometimes carpool to work. Well, he pools, at least. His friend Richie, to Anna's great chagrin, drives a motorcycle. The night of Joe and Jill's rehearsal dinner, when Anna picked up Tony at the Garden State Parkway exit to bring him to church, he arrived on the back of said motorcycle, holding on to Richie's waist.

daily. Trouble followed him everywhere, but he seemed to take everything in stride. The *least* problematic thing Tony faced on a given day would ruin my entire week and render me unable to rise from my pit of despair.

It became evident that Tony was very good at separating his private life from his professional life despite the fact his professional life was constantly calling him on the phone. Granted, this wasn't always the case—I entered the picture at a time when Tony was progressing into a much more balanced and calm human being. Still, his work ethic was nothing if not admirable, his positive attitude nothing if not inspiring.

But what does he actually deal with? What types of problems does he face on a day-to-day basis?

Were it not for being near him when he is discussing work matters on the phone, we probably would know nothing about what he endures on a daily basis. He just doesn't let on. As it is, we know but a fraction of the craziness my father-in-law has faced.

The mortgage and real estate side of things offers little in the way of interesting drama, at least as far as we're concerned. But a major aspect of Tony's job is managing several buildings—he is a landlord. That means he deals with tenants. Brooklyn tenants. Hundreds of them.

I cannot go into exact detail concerning the escapades of said tenants for several reasons, but I can offer some highlights. Keep in mind these are just some things I personally have been privy to throughout the past several years. And believe me, I can relate to all of these incidents because crazy things always happen at my job, too. For example, that time the fax machine broke. That was the worst.

The Businessman

There was the time an ejected tenant demanded Tony help him move his couch out of the apartment. (The man was ejected for having twelve stray cats—*twelve*—that he had, defying his lease agreement, taken into his apartment.) Tony informed the man that was not part of his responsibility as landlord and: no. The next day there was a crusty, cat urine-stained couch blocking the front door to Tony's office with a note that read "I moved it. Thanks for nothing."

There was the time the Brooklyn Police Department called Tony just before midnight to inform him that a drunk had thrown a brick through his office window. "The alarm is going off and there is glass everywhere," the officer said, "which is a risk to passersby. Please get here now." This has happened several times, but the occasion referenced here was Christmas Eve.

There are the many, many times one particular tenant—let's call him Jimmy Wilson, who sleeps during the day and is up at night (not because of any type of "job")—calls Tony's cell phone and leaves messages voicing complaints and offering suggestions as to how the building could be better operated. In doing so, he emphatically uses the phrase "Repeat." His complaints have ranged from there is no heat, to there is too much heat, to the water flow is low, to the hallway is dark: "Tony, it's Jimmy Wilson. Repeat, Jimmy Wilson. I'm in the hallway and can't see a thing, Tony. Repeat: There is not enough light in the hallway. Tell that good-for-nothin' supa to get up here and check the lights! Repeat, this is Jimmy Wilson, hallway is dark, calling at … 3:17 a.m."

There was the time when, after becoming involved in a tenant-landlord dispute for nonpayment of rent, Tony received a letter in the mail asking if he would like to settle the matter in ... *The People's Court*. Like on TV. Despite the desperate pleas of his daughter to please, please, *please* appear on the show, Tony maintained his dignity and declined ... and got his rent money anyway. (I often wonder what would have happened had he appeared on the show, and my guess is that it would have resulted in the most confusing episode ever and/or he would have become an instant D-list celebrity and would be filming season six of his own reality show *right now*.

There was the time Tony received this voice mail message, verbatim, from one of his tenants just days before Christmas: "Tony, it's Mark DeStefano. Listen, Tony, the heat is pretty high, and it's too damn hot in here. I don't know why the heat is so high, but it's really unnecessary. You should think about going green ... lower your carbon imprint, save the planet, all that. So anyway, turn down the f*&^ing heat. Happy holidays."[51]

There was the time, years ago, a Russian woman began pestering Tony about needing her apartment painted. Considering it had just been repainted prior to her moving in, Tony did not think it was necessary. His insistence that it was unnecessary fell on deaf ears, and Tony eventually reverted to avoiding the woman altogether. Unfortunately, Tony's personal office window was visible from the street. Casually looking out the window one day, Tony inadvertently made eye contact with the approaching Russian tenant and was left with nowhere to hide. She barged into the office and dropped

---

[51] Did Monica and I autotune that message by re-recording it on an autotune app, and then play it on an endless loop with great enjoyment? Possibly.

The Businessman

two full gallon paint cans on Tony's desk, making a loud thumping noise and further disheveling a mound of paperwork. Tony was then informed loudly, in a thick Russian accent and with many American curse words, that he now had the materials to paint and no more excuses not to.

As a testament to his fierce principles, Tony did *not* paint the apartment.

Dom the Supa did.

Dom the Supa is the superintendent for the buildings Tony manages. It is true that Tony bravely confronts all the problems of the day head-on, but even he needs help. Whenever something happens, like the A/C goes out or a drunken tenant smashes his not-even-supposed-to-have aquarium and floods the apartment with water and baby piranhas, Tony will immediately call Dom the Supa.

I have never witnessed Tony have a casual conversation with DTS, like "How are you doing?" or "What is your actual last name?" When they communicate, it is always Tony dispensing only the details of what needs to be done, and Dom responding with grunts and yeah okays.

One will rarely witness Tony more frustrated than when a situation has urgency and he cannot get in touch with Dom the Supa. This frustration is due to a) the urgency of the situation, b) Tony's fear that DTS has yet again lost or broken the cell phone Tony gave him (he inherits all of Tony's old phones), and c) Tony essentially views their relationship as a one-way street where DTS should be at his every beck and call. Tony will frequently call Dom the Supa's cell phone incessantly to no avail. He will then be forced to call the office to see if he is there and if he's not, Tony will have someone from the office search under every stone in Brooklyn to find him. When Dom the Supa is finally located, he and Tony will have a conversation not dissimilar to this (I have a grasp on these conversations because they frequently occur on speakerphone while we are all in the car):

"Dom."

Tony hears rustling noises but no answer.

"Dom.

"Dom.

"DOM! Sonofa—"

"Yeah," Dom answers, casually.

"Why didn't you pick up the phone before?"

"What phone? I'm on the phone now."

"Don't play dumb. Your cell phone. The phone I gave you."

"Yeah, uh, what about it?"

"What about it? I called you ON IT seven times."

"..."

"Let me ask you a question. What is the point of me giving you a phone if you're not going to answer it?"

"..."

"Where is it? Did you lose it again?"

"What? Pfft. Nooooo, I didn't lose it."

"Where is it?"

"You know, I uh ... at the moment right now, I uh ... I can't find the charger, and the uh, the battery it's a ... it's a ...

not doing too good. And the phone is kind of broken. On account of me breaking it, by accident."

Tony puts his hand over the speaker of the phone and says to no one in particular, "I swear ... I swear ... "

"It's okay though. Don't worry about it."

"Yeah, don't worry about it my ass. Listen—you remember that apartment I rented three weeks ago to the guy with the eye patch?"

" ... "

"DOM."

"Yeah, eye patch."

"He has no hot water. I also got a call from the Siamese twins in 3C saying the same thing. Listen, I know what it is. Someone keeps turning the switch off for the hot water heater in the boiler room because they think it's a light. By the way, is that *you* doing that?"

"Nah."

"Yeah right it isn't. Go to the boiler room, turn the switch on that's on the far right side of wall, and then install a plastic cover over it so this doesn't happen again, okay?"

" ... "

"Dom."

"Yeah."

"Did you hear what I just said?"

"Yeah."

"You gonna do it?"

"Yeah."

"Call me if there's a problem."

"Yeah. Oh, Ton—"

The Man in the Garlic Tuxedo

Tony has hung up.

Tony has also been known to employ Dom the Supa with non-work-related tasks, such as driving Monica and her friends to Madison Square Garden to see Neil Diamond. On that night Dom the Supa somehow managed to drop them off directly in front of MSG, *on Seventh Avenue,* under the marquee, as if they were celebrities emerging from a '91 Chevy Blazer. That is nearly impossible to do. It's also illegal. So, after the girls exited the vehicle a few cops on foot tried to swarm Dom's car, but he got away. He is, you see, very elusive, yet indispensable for the entire family.

One time Dom the Supa's brother, who is unfortunately not "all there," was caught urinating on the side of the office building. This made for an awkward and sensitive situation, but Tony handled it with class and dignity. He said, "Dom, your brother pissed on the building. You're gonna have to clean that up. Also, I need a ride to Atlantic City."

I do not know what my father-in-law pays Dom the Supa to be his right-hand man—besides the endless stream of outdated cellular phones—but whatever it is, it is not enough.

The Hipster

One evening my in-laws returned home early from what was supposed to be a night at the movies. The film that Tony had spontaneously decided they should see, *Next Friday*, the sequel to *Friday*, starring Ice Cube, had proven to be surprisingly disappointing.

We were all at the house when they returned, and we were awestruck. There were so, so many questions. For example:

Did you even *look* at the movie poster beforehand?

Did the nature of the crowd in the theater give you any indication that this was maybe not a movie targeted at your demographic?

Who goes to the movies without any clue what they're going to see?

What limited knowledge about *Next Friday* swayed your decision?

The Man in the Garlic Tuxedo

I mean, I have seen *Friday* approximately thirty times—like many, I can quote it ad nauseam—and even *I* had no desire to see *Next Friday*. It was fun, however, to picture my in-laws sitting there in the theater as the movie began, trying to process what was happening. My mother-in-law spends a typical day going to church, Wegmans, and brunch, so it's obvious she can relate to the following plotline, courtesy of IMDB:

"Debo has escaped from prison and is looking to get revenge on Craig. So Craig's dad takes him to Rancho Cucamonga to hide out with his Uncle Elroy and cousin Day-Day, who moved to the suburbs after winning the lottery."

All of us wanted to know how long they lasted in the theater before leaving in a huff, but they wouldn't tell us. In fact, Tony didn't even want to talk about it. There is no better indication of Tony's disappointment than when he doesn't want to talk about something.

(Amazingly, this was not their first accidental venture into the realm of African American, marijuana-based comedy. Years ago my mother-in-law, responsible for selecting the right flick from Blockbuster for family movie night, came home with *Half Baked*, a weed comedy starring Dave Chappelle. She assumed it was about a group of guys opening a bakery where everything goes wrong and hijinks ensue. She didn't make it through five minutes, and Tony thankfully fell asleep. But all was not lost, as the movie supplanted the awkward parental "drugs" conversation with Anthony, who was thirteen at the time and now a full-fledged pothead.[52])

---

[52] He is not.

The Hipster

With regard to pop culture, it's not just movies that Tony has an obvious affection for. Like many, he also enjoys music and is frequently on the front lines of questioning the whereabouts of modern singer-songwriters. To be more specific, "What the f&^% happened to Sarah McLachlan?"

That is the question he asked my wife and me from the back seat as we drove my in-laws into the city one day. A Sarah McLachlan song had come on the radio, and Tony, an obvious McLachlan fan—"McLachlanut" is the term, I believe—although we didn't know that until that very moment, was very upset about her ongoing hiatus from music. The force and sheer *profanity* with which he asked the question was in direct contrast to the gentle ease of the Sarah McLachlan song playing on the radio. Unfortunately, neither my wife nor I knew where SML was at the moment, and Tony would have to wait years until her next release, which he did not buy out of spite.

Another late 90s musical act that Tony greatly enjoyed was the Backstreet Boys. The great thing about Tony—and all parents, really—is that he is not bound by the skeptical eye rolls of hipster youth culture. He doesn't really understand the ramifications of the term "boy band," and if he does, he doesn't care. If he hears a song he likes on WPLJ[53], he will buy that artist's album. Then he will play the album in his car very,

---

[53] WPLJ is a NY/NJ metropolitan area pop radio station and also acts as the number one music AND news source for my mother-in-law. Everything Anna knows comes from the *Scott & Todd Morning Show*, and her information is often inaccurate because she doesn't differentiate between the rumors, jokes, actual news, and prank phone calls featured on the program. "Did you hear President Obama got prank called by Frankie Farts-A-Lot yesterday? Ha, yeah well, that's what he GETS for doing the budget like that!"

The Man in the Garlic Tuxedo

very loudly, with the windows rolled down as he pulls up in front of his daughter's NYU dorm to pick her up for the weekend. These were the traumatizing moments she endured in college. The ironic thing is that there are parents out there who would do such a thing ironically (Can an irony be ironic? For the sake of this let's say yes.) as a purposeful attempt to embarrass and humble their children. But I believe Tony was in some small way genuinely trying to show off.

"Check me out! Listening to the hottest tunes! I'm almost sixty but you wouldn't know it! What's up NEW YORK CITY?"

My wife once tried to counter this embarrassment with theft. As Tony dropped her off in front of her dorm one Sunday evening, she discreetly slipped the Backstreet Boys CD into her bag and safely brought it up to her room. On getting there, she excitedly informed her roommates about her successful mission. Five minutes later, there was a knock on the door.

It couldn't be. Security at NYU was *super* tight, and you absolutely required a student ID to get past the gate at the front desk. Even if he had somehow managed to do that, the haggling process would have lasted at least ten minutes, and phone calls would certainly have been made to the room. It just couldn't be.

It was. When Monica answered the door, he said only this:

"Give me my Backstreet Boys CD back. I want to listen to it on the way home."

Like his penchant for cooking, Tony's love of music truly manifests itself during the holidays, specifically New Year's

The Hipster

Eve. Every year for his NYE party that consists of seven hours of eating and thirty minutes of party time, Tony will stock up on what he describes as "party mix CDs." These albums have titles like *Party Mix 3000, Bumpin' Beats, Now That's What I Call New Year's Eve Vol. XXII, Booty Club Mix—Parental Advisory Version* (mistake purchase) and *Bilingual Club Hits—Italian/English* and they mostly consist of anonymous singers covering popular songs.

About twenty minutes or so before the ball drops, Tony will put one of his party mix CDs into the stereo and bump it way too loudly, at which point Anna will yell at him to turn it down. He will, slightly, and while wearing a party hat and glasses that spell out the upcoming year, Tony will dance to a fake version of "Who Let the Dogs Out?" while Uncle Carmine sleeps on the couch and everyone else talks amongst themselves.

According to Monica, one of those CDs from the late 90s featured a fake club version of "I Want It That Way," Tony's favorite.

Which reminds me, what the f^%$ happened to the Backstreet Boys?

The Handyman

There are many men who are handier than me, and that includes every man who has ever existed. My dad is a plumber/pipefitter and can do lots of other things, none of which were passed down to me genetically.[54] My neighbor Ron can build a gun from scratch, although I'm pretty sure he once killed a bear using only his teeth. As previously mentioned, my father-in-law is also very handy.

There is, however, one man who trumps them all: Uncle Carmine. My wife's uncle is the handiest person I know. There is nothing he cannot fix, build, or figure out.

---

[54] Once when I was in grammar school I scored the role of "shepherd" in a Christmas play, and my only costume requirements were a bedsheet and a staff. The next day my dad came home with a six-foot-tall steel staff, curled at the end, that he made himself at work. I'm not sure it was historically accurate, but I was the envy of all the other shepherds. Picturing him wearing a protective mask and wielding a blowtorch so that his son would be the baddest ass shepherd crowding around the baby Jesus makes me proud to call him my dad.

The Man in the Garlic Tuxedo

Uncle Carmine is a quiet, reserved man. He is originally from Italy, and when he does speak he does so in a strong Italian accent that is sometimes unintelligible to the average American. He drives a gray van, smokes Marlboro Reds, and sometimes has woodchips in his hair. Nothing concerns him. The world could be collapsing in on itself, and there would be Uncle Carmine smoking a cigarette while taking apart a carburetor.

His full-time trade is landscaping, but he does it all. Tony himself has perfectly described Uncle Carmine's motivation and general working style as "He sees a lawn and he cuts it." That pretty much sums it up. No frills, just execution. Whenever something needs to be done, we call Uncle Carmine.[55]

Even Tony will call on the technical genius of his brother-in-law, which is the surest sign of his respect for Carmine's know-how. However, that does not mean he completely trusts Carmine because my father-in-law completely trusts no man. Instead, they will do the job together.

When Tony and Uncle Carmine work together on a project, it makes for a magnificent case study and extremely entertaining event for the rest of the family. It's better to be discreet by feigning attempts to assist them, but I would prefer that we could all pull up chairs and eat popcorn and watch them work. I am not sure there are two men with more in common—from Italy, brothers-in-law, same exact height—with more contrasting personalities and working styles. Their relationship is not unlike the one between Tony and Dom the

---

[55] It should be mentioned that Uncle Carmine *does* have one area of interest that transcends work, and that is watching interplanetary and space specials on the Discovery Channel. This means he is either head-down in mindless, thankless, hard labor, or contemplating the complexities of the universe. There is no in-between.

The Handyman

Supa, with Tony's attempts to exert his authority met with an unmatched level of both patience and indifference. The only thing they share while working is a mutual disregard for directions—Uncle Carmine because he works by sight and touch, Tony because directions don't know what the heck they're talking about.

The following is a hypothetical transcript of such an occasion, based on many of the times we have witnessed them work together:

Tony and Uncle Carmine stare at the project in front of them.

"Okay," Tony says. "Carmine, go out to the van and get your circular saw."

Uncle Carmine goes outside, smokes a cigarette, and comes back with nothing.

"Where is the saw?" Tony asks.

"Ehhh," Uncle Carmine responds, "don't think we need it."

"What?"

"It's like, look ... *(picks up piece of wood, breaks it with bare hands, shaves it down to scale with his fingernails)* ... right?"

"Mother of ... it can't work like that! Do you see where it has to fit over there? I measured it beforehand. It has to be exactly three and seven-eighths inches wide or it's not going to fit."

Uncle Carmine places the piece of wood into the groove, and it fits perfectly.

"See," Uncle Carmine says, "like this. Right?"

"That is not to be believed. Alright, where is the plastic tubing?"

The Man in the Garlic Tuxedo

Uncle Carmine is still staring at the piece of wood he has placed down.

"Carmine?"

Uncle Carmine shrugs.

"Did you pick up the plastic tubing at Home Depot like I asked you to yesterday?"

"Ehhh ... they didn't have it."

"Home Depot didn't have plastic tubing? Did you look in the plastic tubing aisle?"

"They uh ... didn't have the right one, right?"

Tony shakes his head.

"S'okay, s'okay," Uncle Carmine reassures Tony.

"How is this okay? There is literally nothing we can do without the plastic tubing."

Uncle Carmine leaves, comes back thirty-five minutes later with plastic tubing.

"Carmine ... wha ... where the hell have you been?"

"Ehh ... Home Depot. *(laughs, coughs)*"

"Alright, I know how we have to do this. Give me a piece of the three-quarter inch ... set it down here ... hold it there like this. Now, let me just ... *(tries to do something, doesn't work)* What the ... ? Carmine, are you holding it right?"

Uncle Carmine does not respond.

"If you don't hold it right, it's not going to work!" Tony yells. "Try it again, and this time make sure you hold it like I told you."

Tony tries it again. It doesn't work.

"I don't think you got the right tubing," Tony says, defeated. "This cannot be the right tubing."

"It's right, right?"

"You smell like smoke, and it's making me sick. I can't do this with you smelling like that."[56]

Uncle Carmine does not respond to the accusation of smelliness.

"I don't know what you did," Tony says while sweating profusely.

"Here, let me try," Carmine says. "Not horizontal, got to be vertical *(holds up tube)*, right? Like this ... *(inserts piece of tubing, snaps in place)* Right?"

"That ... that can't be. *(checks tubing)* That's not gonna hold."

"Oh yeah, it'll hold. Watch ... *(grabs on to tubing, hangs from it, suspended in air, cigarette hanging out of mouth like Vince Vaughn on the rings in* Old School*)* Right?"

"That is not to be believed."

Uncle Carmine laughs, then coughs. The cough turns violent, and he hocks something up that makes a clinking noise as it hits the floor. It turns out to be a screw.

"I was looking for that," Tony says. "We need that."

---

[56] Tony has a very keen and very sensitive sense of smell. One time we walked in and out of a restaurant because he said he could "smell the oil they use to cook," and he didn't approve.

The Beast

It's not just Tony's work ethic that's remarkable. His leisure ethic is equally impressive.

Saying that my father-in-law lives an active lifestyle would seem to imply that he gets out three times a week for bocce ball at the community center. No, no, no. Tony is active to the point of insanity, and there is nothing that can stop him.

He is a beast.

Part of this is how he is wired. He physically cannot stop doing things. He is like some sort of human experiment who will die if he stops moving. He is the movie *Speed* of people. No person can claim he ever witnessed my father-in-law sitting in a recliner, scratching himself while having a beer and watching a spelling bee on TV.[57]

He is also motivated. By health, yes, but also by defying

---

[57] That is my idea of sloth and excess.

The Man in the Garlic Tuxedo

age and proving to himself over and over again that he can hang with the young guns. Sometimes this is comical.

Years ago we were at a wedding for my wife's friend, and my in-laws were also invited. I don't like to brag, but I have developed a reputation for dancing like a complete moron and embarrassing myself at weddings. I was doing just that at this wedding—The Running Man to be specific—in the middle of a circle with everybody clapping and laughing. Tony became overly excited at what was happening, and began to try to mimic the already poorly performed dance I was doing. It may have been the European version of The Running Man he was attempting, although it seemed many aspects of the original were lost in translation. After about ten seconds he completely lost control of his body. His limbs were flying everywhere, he lost his balance, and came very close to falling down. What saved him from falling was the fact that he had knocked into one of the DJ's gigantic speakers, which was resting on a pedestal. The speaker rocked back and forth, about to violently topple over, threatening guests and the all-glass window/wall that overlooked the outdoor patio of the reception hall. Thankfully, a few of us rushed over to the wobbling speaker and secured it just in time. I don't want to say the wedding would have been ruined if the speaker had fallen over, but—yeah, it pretty much would have been ruined.[58]

So yes, it can be comical. More often than not, however,

---

[58] Tony would considerably improve his wedding dance moves. At our wedding—after taking actual *lessons* during which he had to follow an instructor's directions (!)—he and Monica performed a surprise tango and swing dance to Louis Prima's "Buena Sera Signorina" for their father-daughter dance. They were great.

The Beast

Tony succeeds in proving he's still got it. More often than not, we are truly mystified by his physical stamina.

How does he do it?

He is Italian, so there is only one answer—food.

Tony creates what the family can only describe as "concoctions," and no matter what he puts in them, they are always green. I think it's the wheatgrass. What is wheatgrass? I do not know. I *do* know that when you combine it with flaxseed oil, oatmeal, organic bananas, rice milk, fish oil, crushed digestive vitamins, actual grass, ginseng leaves, and soybeans from Wegmans, you get something that no human being should ever look at, much less ingest. When Tony makes one of these concoctions using a blender, the ensuing mess makes it appear as though several wild animals invaded the kitchen, knocked a bunch of stuff over, and then got sick all over the counter.

But it works. His dedicated if not bizarre diet plan enables Tony to do things like take daily spinning classes at the gym. Or, better yet, run a spinning class. Indeed, one time he conducted a spinning class when the instructor called out sick. I know. I was there. It was amazing. He wore a headset and yelled instructions like, "Do it now! Bike!" to the class in his Italian accent while in front of a giant projection screen featuring images of various bike-riding landscapes.

Tony is an avid golfer. Golf is generally considered a sport of leisure, but Tony defies that notion. When he and the boys go on their annual golf vacation, they golf two rounds a day, every day, for a week. I did have the honor of joining them on a golf vacation, only it happened to be during an unbearable East Coast summer heat wave. It's difficult to refrain from hyperbole when describing extreme weather, but I assure you I am not exaggerating when I say it was one hundred degrees each day with a humidity of one million percent. Daily public safety reports said, "Stay inside, idiots." Going out to golf in that weather was borderline suicidal, and we were playing TWO ROUNDS per day. The daily latter round was in the extreme afternoon heat, during which we were often the only group on the course. Joe and I were in our twenties, Anthony was still a teenager, and we barely survived it. Anthony almost collapsed at dinner one evening. Every day, however, there was Tony, near sixty, humming along, more concerned with what club he should use than the fact that it felt like we were golfing in hell.

Tony is an avid tennis player. Though he is much better than I am, we are very evenly matched because my long reach works in my favor. He is a smart man's tennis player—he hits everything to the perfect spot and runs me ragged all over the court. We've had some epic matches. One day we were playing, and something wasn't right. I was beating him rather convincingly, and he just wasn't getting to balls he normally would.

"Dad, you okay?" I said.

"Yeah, yeah, I'm fine. I'm fine," he replied.

We continued to play. Now he was limping.

"Dad, are you sure you're okay?"

"Yeah, I'm fine. My calf is just a little … I'm fine. Your serve."

"We can stop now, ya' know."

"NO! SERVE!"

I felt bad, so I started hitting the ball to where he was standing so he didn't have to move around as much. Sure enough, he started landing shots and running me all over the

The Beast

court. Eventually I said, "Screw it," and started playing normal again. I'm not sure what it says about me that I felt the need to defeat my sixty-year-old, injured father-in-law at tennis, but he drove me to that point. After the match I looked at his calf, which had blown up to the size of Serena Williams's thigh. Only when it was decided we were finished playing did he admit his calf-thigh was bothering him. "Ya' think?" I said as I stared at it in disbelief. He decided he should jog home to "run it off."[59]

Because Tony is a runner. As a family, we run a lot of road races together. My parents are avid runners too, and we can usually recruit other family members to run or walk a road race if there is the promise of beer afterward. Tony need not be convinced, although he will frequently forget to register for a race in time yet somehow get in post-deadline.

Road races combine two of Tony's favorite pastimes: being active and technology. Every technological device he has ever owned is a must-have on race day. GPS, iPod, iPhone, watch, GPS watch, iPhone GPS app, running glasses that tell you how far you've gone, pedometer, digital fanny pack, headband with satellite antennae, etc. It doesn't matter that the iPhone itself can pretty much do everything, or that the race typically provides trackers—race day reaffirms that all of his prior technological purchases were wise ones. At one race in particular, he became entangled in the wires of his devices while trying to put his headband on, and Monica had to get the knots out and release him into the starting corral.

---

[59] This did not work.

The Man in the Garlic Tuxedo

Then there is the race itself. Here is how race day has gone for every single race we have ever run together:

"Yeah, Mike, what corral are you in again? Oh yeah? Think I'll go in that one, too. It's not the one they assigned me, but they don't know anything. Listen, I don't care about my time, so you just keep the pace, okay? It's better that we stay together, you know? I'm going to follow you, don't worry about me. But if you want to go ahead, if you're feeling it, feeling good, go right ahead. We'll meet under the giant inflatable 5-Hour Energy drink afterward like we talked about, right? That's where we're meeting, right? But that's just in case … I think we should stay together. I'm going to follow you. You keep the pace."

Then the gun goes off and he is gone. *Gone.* Full on sprint, no-looking-back, gone. The time elapsed from him finishing that spiel to him being one hundred yards ahead of me or anyone he has promised to stay with is fewer than five seconds.

Every time. Every. Time.

He's completed multiple half-marathons. He's participated in bike-riding events, and he attends his spin class religiously. Oh, and he sails. Like he will spend multiple days on a sailboat in the middle of the ocean as a means of enjoyment. Once, he and three other guys spent weeks sailing down the East Coast. Here is how my mother-in-law informed Monica of that situation:

"You wanna know where your fatha is? He's sailing down to Florida with Frank and two schmoes I don't even know. They got one bed on the boat and your fatha's on night duty. He might be home in March, he says. Don't even get me started."

The Great Communicator

One of Tony's most awe-inspiring talents, as mentioned, is his ability to identify a person's ethnicity. The specificity with which he is able to pinpoint a complete stranger's homeland based on factors like appearance, accent, mannerisms, and nature of employment—"You'd be surprised how many Angolans work in boat supply sales"—is unrivaled, yet understandable. After all, the man has been all around the world and has prided himself on his ability to interact with people of different cultures and backgrounds.

Less understandable and in total contrast to his ability to nail an ethnicity is his utter inability to recall people's actual, human names. But hey, a lot of people aren't the best at remembering names, and many comedic anecdotes have been uttered with regard to the awkward situation of being unable to recall a person's name during a conversation. We've all been there. Tony, however—I hope this book is driving home this theme—is different. Not being able to remember a person's name does not often deter him from calling that person *a name*. For Tony, having to ask a person his name is, apparently, infinitely more embarrassing than just taking a shot in the dark.

He struggles with names on land.

"Hello, sir, what can I get for you today?" said the Dunkin' Donuts employee.

"Oh boy, 'sir,' huh?" Tony replied. "Well I'm not *that* old. So hey there ... *(squints to read employee's nametag)* ... 'Peter.'"

Tony was visibly proud of himself for taking the time to learn the young man's identity as opposed to just treating him like a nameless employee.

"Ummm," Peter said while looking down at his nametag, then back up at Tony, "that says 'James.' Name is James."

"'James?' Are you sure? I don't know, I don't have my glasses. I just ... *(fumbles for wallet)* listen—is the decaf fresh? Don't lie to me, Peter. Also, I would like the senior citizen discount."

Anthony was present when Tony called "his guy Ben" to pick up him and Anna and take them to the airport. Anthony then sent me the following text:

> Dad on the phone: "yeah hi Ben" ... Pause while Ben talks. "yeah ok yeah oh Ron ok I used you a few weeks ago to go to Newark." Lol

The Great Communicator

He struggles with names in the air.

"Excuse me, Christie?" Tony said to the flight attendant. The flight attendant did not turn around.

"Excuse me ... CHRISTIE?" Tony said.

The flight attendant turned around slowly, seeming confused, made eye contact with Tony, and pointed to herself.

"Are you calling for me?" she asked.

"Yes, Christie, I am. Listen, I'm a club member, so please tell me—why does this movie cost $6.99?"

"Okaaaaay, actually, for starters, my name is Darcy."

"Oh, Darcy, yeah. I don't know ... I heard you talking before, and thought you said your name was Christie."

"Maybe that was Chris, our other flight attendant?"

Darcy pointed to Chris, a man.

"Maybe, I don't know," Tony said. "I thought you were Christie. You're not Christie though?"

"No. As far as the movie goes, it costs the same for club and non-club members alike."

"That is just ... not to be believed. I'm not even sure why I'm a club member. I thought I would just watch *The Curious Case of Ben's Buttons*, but I guess not."

He struggles with names on water.

Years ago, Tony, Anthony, cousin Sal, and I went on a white water rafting trip sponsored by the local church youth group. It was a very adventurous time in all of our lives. The entire group gathered around the trip's guide as she explained

The Man in the Garlic Tuxedo

all the dos and don'ts of white water rafting. Then, we were off.

We had all departed from shore and were floating quietly along the river in our respective rafts, anxiously awaiting the rough waters ahead. Everyone involved was taking it all in, enjoying the pleasant sounds of nature. Tony, giddy from being on a youth-based outdoor adventure, interrupted the serenity when he stood[60], spotted our guide leading another raft about fifty yards ahead of us, waved, and yelled at the top his lungs, "Hi, Mary!"

Mary smiled, waved back and, after a brief pause that we later determined to be her weighing whether or not it was even worth it, yelled back across the river, "My name is Nancy!"

Although Anna is, like all of us, frequently befuddled by the exploits of her husband and generally acts as the number one Tony apologist, she is little help with the name problem.[61] Any name, person, or thing longer than two syllables will often force her to violently sound it out, only to give up at the end.

"I was listening to *Scott & Todd* today," Anna said, "and

---

[60] Rule number two during preadventure presentation: Do not stand up in the raft.
[61] The name problem certainly doesn't just involve everyday white people names. My in-laws' neighbor in Arizona is African American. His name is by no means complicated or even unusual, but it is definitely not "Frank." It is also not "Dermon," "Delmon," "Drum-man,"(!) or any of the other names Tony has actually called him. I do believe Anna went through the trouble of writing his name down on a piece of paper and posting it on the refrigerator. This has helped immensely on the occasions that Tony has run into his neighbor on his way to the fridge, which so far has been zero times.

they were talking about what's her name ... Kim ... KARD-ISH-O-DISH-A-ganiganorwhateva."

"MA!" Monica said. "Are you serious?"

Language in general is sometimes a struggle for my in-laws, because they both suffer from the dreaded S-disease.

I had never known about the S-disease until I became a part of their family, but it is not to be taken lightly. Aptly named by all four of their children, the S-disease is when you uncontrollably add *s* to the end of a noun that does not end in *s* and conversely remove the *s* from nouns that do end in *s*.

You can imagine the horror and confusion that have resulted from this rare but terrible disease.

"Tony," Anna said, "we're late! I told you I had to go to Kohl."

"Kohl?" Tony said. "I thought we were going to Targets."

"We have to go there, too. Whateva the case, we better get home quick cause I'm not missing *Ellens*. She's gonna have on Billy Joels. I hope he sings 'Piano Mans.'"

"Are we still going out to Drew in Keyports for dinner?"

"Tomorrah. Tonight we're driving into Staten Islands and going to Paul."

The Family Man

We all—cousins, aunts, uncles, etc.—went into the city a few days before Christmas to see a show. We met at Uncle Paul's house in Staten Island and took the bus to NYC.

It was lightly drizzling the entire day, but after the show it was a full-fledged rain. The plan was for us to take the bus back to Staten Island, order a bunch of pizzas for dinner, and unwind at the house. We huddled together at the bus stop, trying not to hit one another with umbrellas. We were cold, wet, and very hungry after a long day in the city. We waited and waited. After a long while of no bus arriving, we double-checked the miniscule bus sign nearby, which informed us that the transportation authority had recently changed the bus route. We were at the wrong stop.

We trudged however many blocks it was to the correct stop. Now we were cold, wet, hungry, frustrated, and annoyed. Considering the time of day it had now become—five p.m. on a weekday—there was concern as to whether or not all of us would even fit on the bus once it arrived. We were all on edge. Especially Tony.

As we waited, a group of loud and obnoxious teenagers arrived. Maybe they weren't *so* loud and obnoxious, but their moods were in direct contrast to ours, so our agitation was heightened. They also had situated themselves in front of our group and close to the sidewalk curb. There's no real line at a bus stop, but they had essentially cut us in line. Considering there were seventeen of us waiting to board a bus together back to Staten Island, this was cause for concern.

Tony had been giving them the stink-eye from the start. He was also muttering things like, "freakin' kids … loudmouths … I'll be darned … bus jerks." The teenagers were doing little to help their case, cursing loudly, hitting one another, and generally attempting to put out the vibe of intimidation and invincibility for which teenagers in the public sphere are quite famous.

Finally, the bus arrived, its approaching headlights piercing the rain and evening sky, giving us hope and relief.

Sure enough, the kids inched closer to the curb and situated themselves to where they thought the bus doors would open. Possibly they were very experienced with this particular bus, since their guess as to where it would stop proved accurate. They attempted to form a wall, ensuring they'd be first to board.

My father-in-law closed his umbrella and said to the rest of us, "Okay, follow my lead." With that he approached the group of teenagers, turned around so that his backside was facing them, squatted slightly, outstretched his arms, and backed into them, pushing them back and out of the way.

The bus released a puff of exhaust and opened its doors, inviting us in. Tony said, "Alright, get on NOW! Go, go, go! No questions—NOW!"

The group of teenagers was now behind the wall of Tony, unable to fully grasp what was happening and yelling things like, "Dude, you're crazy! Get off me! Is this even happening right now? This is ridiculous!" The male teenagers, just minutes ago so brazen in front of their female friends, were now trying to awkwardly laugh off the fact they were being physically held back by a 5'8" sixty-two-year-old man while trying to board a city bus.

All of us boarded, moving swiftly past Tony while trying not to make eye contact with the teenagers yelling behind him. The rain poured on my father-in-law as he mustered all his strength to make a pathway for us to freedom. It felt like we were trying to escape a violent civil rights protest about to erupt, and I honestly thought I might get spit on. I actually wasn't sure whether to board or wait with Tony in case the kids attempted to return the physicality. I had visions of returning to work the following week with a black eye and informing my coworkers, "I went to see *Spamalot* with my father-in-law over the holidays and we ended up getting into a brawl with a bunch of high school kids." So I boarded.

The last to board was Uncle Carmine who, seemingly oblivious to everything that was happening, motioned for Tony to go ahead of him. Tony, still struggling to hold back a small angry mob of kids, nodded toward the bus. Uncle Carmine put his hand on Tony's shoulder and insisted he go first.

The Man in the Garlic Tuxedo

It wasn't as if Uncle Carmine was pleading with his brother-in-law on behalf of the kids—it truly seemed like he didn't even notice what Tony was doing and was just trying to be a gentleman. Nevertheless, the delay in boarding put Tony at risk of getting trampled, so he yelled, "GET ON THE BUS, CARMINE!" Uncle Carmine shrugged and walked on.

We were all seated when Tony walked on. Of course it turned out there was plenty of room for everybody, so one by one the group of kids filed onto the bus directly behind Tony, still jabbering insults at him the whole way. "You're crazy, man!"

Tony stopped his walk down the bus aisle, looked up at the ceiling, shook both of his fists in the air, and said, "YOU WANT TO SEE CRAZY? I'LL SHOW YOU CRAZY!" Then he winked at all of us and sat down next to Anna.

When the bus pulled away we all looked at one another wide-eyed, paralyzed by what had just happened. My wife was slumped in her seat from embarrassment. Tony was already reading a magazine as if nothing had happened.

There were still taunting murmurs from the front seats, but my father-in-law could not have cared less. The family was on the bus, and that's all that mattered.

Suddenly, Tony turned around in his seat to face the rest of us, and we figured maybe he was going to address what had just happened. Instead he said, "Okay, who's ready for some pizza and wine?" and clapped and rubbed his hands together excitedly.

The Family Man

When Monica and I first started dating in May 2001, she dropped the bomb on me that she'd be leaving that summer to attend Northern Arizona University in Flagstaff, Arizona, to get her master's degree in speech pathology. It was a summers-only graduate program, so it would only be for a couple months.

I decided I would visit her there, which I did that summer and every summer thereafter for the next three years. Flagstaff was beautiful, and we'd make trips down to Phoenix to see a ballgame, and visit the red rocks of Sedona. We loved Arizona and talked about moving there someday.

Besides vehemently fighting its HOA fees, Tony had helped us find and settle into our beloved two-bedroom condo. It was cozy, had a fireplace, and Joe and Jill would soon move in right around the corner. Eventually, however, we thought it was time to leave for something bigger, and we tasked Tony to help us find a single-family home in our modest budget that wasn't a fixer-upper because I cannot fixer-up anything.

There wasn't much. It seemed like every weekend we were out looking at a place we either couldn't afford or couldn't afford to renovate. The fall months turned to winter, and our frustrations mounted as the weather got colder and the days got shorter.

One Sunday night, after another weekend of efforts to find a new home had proved fruitless, Monica and I pulled into our assigned parking spot of the condo development. It was cold, wet, dark, and rainy. Almost simultaneously, we turned to each other and said, "Let's move to Arizona."

The only thing that had been holding us back up until

The Man in the Garlic Tuxedo

that point was leaving our family, and although that huge CON remained, all the other PROs—weather, cost of living, weather, open spaces, weather, the weather—were impossible to ignore.

Most everyone feigned support for our decision, not because we were making the wrong one, but because it meant we were leaving. We understood.

There were exceptions, and Tony was one of them. Not that he wanted to see us go either, but he appreciated our adventurous spirit and saw the same positives we did. After all, this was a man who had left everything behind on multiple occasions to see what else the world had to offer, and his background inspired Monica and me to move forward.

Besides, Tony figured, this would enable him to visit Arizona more often. He and the boys had spent one of their golf vacations a few years back in Scottsdale, and they loved it. He wouldn't have to wait long to get back to the desert, accompanying us on an initial trip out there to look for a home, and then going back with me a month later. And we did find a home—one we never would have been able to afford in New Jersey.

With Monica more than two thousand miles away and placing her trust in me and her dad[62] to find the right home, I sat there next to my father-in-law and signed the builder's paperwork. In speaking with the sales rep, Tony had uncovered a considerable builder's incentive, but he had kept that information to himself. When the paper listing the final sale price was slid to me from across the table, I looked at it in

---

[62] Mostly her dad. Only her dad.

shock, and then I looked at Tony as if to say "Is this correct?" He smiled from ear to ear, genuinely happy for us. I'm convinced his mere presence got us that deal.

In fact, Tony helped us with everything, from selling our condo to finding the right mortgage broker to dealing with inspections to physically helping us pack and move. On our second trip out west, he even drove me to—and waited in the rental car during—my two-hour job interview at the local community paper, a job I ending up getting and still have to this day.[63]

From an abstract standpoint, Tony had lived a life that served as an inspiration for us to make the move. From a tangible standpoint, he did everything to ensure that we could and would. We literally couldn't have done it without him.

---

[63] At the end of the interview, the publisher and my future boss Bill said, "Wait, your father-in-law has been outside in the car this whole time? Oh my gosh, I'm so sorry." I said, "Don't worry, he's fine." When I got out to the car, I discovered that Tony had closed two real estate deals over the phone, took a twenty-minute walk to "familiarize himself with his surroundings," during which he "almost got a haircut," set up the next morning's tee time and, after a lot of thought, decided where we would go for dinner: P.F. Chang's.

Arizona

Tony and Anna would visit, staying with us for a week's time or more. When we went to work, Tony would golf while Anna watched the house, keeping herself busy sewing our damaged clothes, doing laundry, and getting new ideas from the Food Network. They cooked dinner every night they stayed, and we often ate outside at our backyard patio table, enjoying the beautiful fall desert weather while catching up on all the family-related drama from back east.

They could, however, never get their bearings when it came to the time-zone change. Arizona proudly doesn't observe daylight saving time, so we're either two or three hours behind Eastern Standard depending on the season. This simple reality has yet to be grasped by my in-laws.

Whether we're talking to her from Arizona or she's in Arizona trying to call someone else, Anna does not know what time it is "there." Monica will say, "Ma, it's the winter, so it's two hours." Anna will then count numbers in her head and say, "Behind or ahead?" Monica will say, "MA! It's always behind!" And then Anna will become too flustered and give up on trying to figure it out. At this very moment, wherever she is, my mother-in-law does not know what time it is there.

Tony knows the time, thanks in no small part to the fact that he purchased an "Arizona watch" that he wears with his East Coast watch—yes, he wears them simultaneously—so he can get business done while on vacation. When he combines these with his third watch—his GPS golf watch that tells him how far ahead the pin is—his arm looks like the wall of clocks in the New York Stock Exchange that display the times throughout the world.

But while he knows the time in his mind, his body does not. No matter how long he's been in Arizona, whether it's been an hour or two weeks, Tony claims his body is "still on East Coast time."

What this means is that Tony is up at ungodly hours in Arizona, even more ungodly than usual. On several occasions during their visits, I found myself having to get up in the middle of the night because our dog was crying to go out. As I tiredly trudged down the stairs, I'd find Tony at the kitchen table working on his laptop.

"Dad," I'd say, "what are you doing up? It's one in the morning."

"Yeah, but for me it's already four a.m. East Coast time," he'd say.

"Dad, you've been in Arizona for three weeks, and four in the morning is *still* ridiculous!"

"I made some coffee. You want some?"

I had a good opportunity to take advantage of Tony's penchant for rising early.

A boot camp was making its way to our part of Arizona, and the organizers reached out to our newspaper to let us know their whole deal. The special boot camp session would be held at University of Phoenix Stadium, home of the Arizona Cardinals and where my beloved New York Giants had recently won the Super Bowl. I thought it would be neat to attend the boot camp, be inside the stadium, on the field where history was made, and write about it for the paper. Tony and Anna were visiting at the time, and I asked my father-in-law if he wanted to join me. I knew he would.

We had to get up at four a.m. just to make it in time for the five a.m. start, which was no problem for at least one of us.

Once we got inside the stadium we realized almost the entire boot camp was middle-aged women. I guess it wasn't apparent to me from the press release what demographic this boot camp was trying to reach.

Not that we're above any sort of exercise, but there we were, two half-marathon veterans, doing stretches and jumping jacks alongside a bunch of women with Curves memberships. Tony continued to perform each exercise long after the instructor had informed us to stop, in a desperate attempt to work up a sweat so his morning wasn't wasted. He had, after all, canceled his tee time for this.

The climax of the boot camp was running up and down the stadium steps, which actually did increase our heart rate a bit. When we went up the first flight of steps and reached the concourse, we saw that the local Channel 12 news was there filming the boot camp for a live feature segment. Tony couldn't have been more excited. He worked himself into the background—he was wearing his signature workout headband, by the way—and waved, laughed, gave thumbs up, and generally acted like the type of person we've all seen in the background of news segments. You know, the person from whom the cameraman has to immediately pan away.

I needed to head off to work after camp, but we had some time so Tony suggested we go out to breakfast. We sat there at the small breakfast table, coffees in hand and the sun still barely up, two men who had just completed what amounted to a jazzercise class. We laughed as we recounted the events of the morning.

Tony then turned to me and said, "You know, Mike, here's the thing—I'm ready to be a grandparent now."

My wife is the oldest sibling in an Italian family, which would normally mean that children would soon if not immediately follow her marriage. There was, however, no such pressure on us. In fact, if there was any pressure it was the pressure *not* to have kids. Not because anyone deemed us not ready, but because my father-in-law was not ready. He was not ready to be labeled a grandparent by society.

Tony has always been hung up on age. As long as I have known him, his life has been best defined by his refusal to admit that time has passed. I've mentioned before that there are certain things not to joke with him about, and his age is definitely one of those things. We celebrated his fifty-ninth birthday for three years straight, and I'm not talking in a ha-ha, wink-wink, type of way. We literally had to pretend he was turning fifty-nine. The commitment that he and my mother-in-law invest in this charade is extraordinary.

Arizona

For Tony, becoming a grandfather was the final plateau. Sure, great-grandfather is a possibility, but not exactly the norm. Being a grandfather was a label he wouldn't be able to escape. He would be forced to admit that time had won. His reluctance to reach that plateau was fine by us since we wanted some time for ourselves after getting married.

To hear him say he was ready to be a grandfather was shocking on several levels. For starters, he said it out of nowhere as I was biting into an egg and cheese biscuit. Also, what had accounted for the seemingly swift change of heart? The bold statement, "I'm ready to be a grandfather," was followed by an awkward silence—mostly because I was chewing—which seemed to imply, at least to me, " ... sooooo, get on that." *That* being making a baby with his daughter. This was all happening at McDonald's.

Tony went on to admit he had been experiencing secondhand the pure joy his dear friends Frank and Jane were experiencing due to grandparenthood. He saw their renewed zest for life at having a grandchild, and he had decided that the joy must far outweigh the label. He was ready now, and thus the pressure was on.

"Ummm, okay, I'll let her know you're ready," was all I could say, as I took another bite.

The truth is that Monica and I had already started talking about becoming parents—foster parents.

Through her job as a speech therapist, Monica worked with several foster and adoptive families. She introduced me to one extraordinary family in particular, who would become our close friends. They had fostered then adopted eight kids, and their home on the day I first met them at a Fourth of July party was like the United Nations of Joy. We fell in love with the idea of foster care (with hopes to adopt) and went for it.

Tony and Anna weren't exactly thrilled about it. Not because they didn't think it was a worthwhile or righteous decision, but because they worried about the logistics and emotions of it all. In Arizona on our own, we had little help minus a few friends and short, sporadic family visits. Would we be able to handle it? Sure, it sounded like a valiant attempt at love and social justice, but what about the realities of foster care? Would our hearts break? How do you give a child back, especially when you have no child of your own? Why didn't we start our family first and *then* consider helping others?

Our minds, however, were already made up. We knew Tony and Anna were only considering what was best for us, and I also suspected they would fall head over heels for any child in our care. In fact, I thought maybe they were as worried about their own emotional attachments as they were about ours.

It was my mom who was in town when we had to return our first foster placement to the social worker, a baby boy we had for ten days. It was heartbreaking, and we felt blindsided despite everything we had learned throughout the licensing process. It was, however, comforting that family was there to see us through.

A few months later we received another placement, a two-year-old girl and her three-month-old brother. They were with us for almost seven months, and when Tony and Anna came for their annual fall visit, they were finally able to meet them in person. Sure enough they fell in love, just as my own parents had months earlier. Tony accompanied Monica to several of the little guy's doctor visits. Anna helped our foster daughter find a Halloween costume, and they spent plenty of time snuggled on the couch reading stories. Tony and I went to church one Saturday evening in the nearby retirement community of Sun City with the little guy in tow. Our foster son was the hit of Mass, and Tony was like a proud grandfather, letting all the nice folks carrying oxygen tanks kiss the baby boy.

Not long after Tony and Anna left for New Jersey, the two little ones were scheduled to go back to their family. The week leading up to their return home, we received a call from our licensing worker. Months earlier we had been sent a file about a baby girl who was available for adoption, and we confirmed our interest and had our licensing worker send our family file. We had never heard back. Well, until now. We were chosen to be the adoptive parents of a three-month-old girl.

It was Thanksgiving Day 2009 when we informed our respective parents of the news. They were going to be grandparents, Tony and Anna for the first time. Everyone was ecstatic, of course. Coincidentally or not, my in-laws had been thinking ... maybe they should get a second home.

In Arizona.

Babbo

After the holidays, Matt, God bless his soul, drove with his parents across the country to their new house in Arizona, three blocks from ours. Tony and Anna would be settling in and staying for a month, and more visitors were on the way. Matt's girlfriend Maureen would soon fly into town, then Anthony. My mom after that. Everyone wanted to meet the girl.

When we pulled up, they had just arrived at the new house after a three-day, cross-country trip with a car packed with things to unload. We got out of the car and presented my in-laws with their granddaughter. Anna scooped her up and didn't let go.

It wasn't the way they had envisioned becoming grandparents, but it didn't take longer than a split second of looking into that little girl's eyes for them to embrace her as their own

The Man in the Garlic Tuxedo

in a sea of unconditional love and immediately side with her on all matters of life.

We adopted our daughter several months later, the summer of 2010. Tony and Anna came back to Arizona for the court hearing.

By the time she was officially our daughter, my father-in-law had long since become the delirious pile of grandfatherly mush he had only recently aspired to be.

Babbo is loosely translated from Italian to English as "dad," but is occasionally—as I have been told—used in Italian-American culture for grandfathers.[64] Tony is now Babbo. I believe it is a term that truly befits the man, since most non-Italians are unfamiliar with the name and are more often than not confused by it, just as they're confused by the man himself. Tony has embraced life as Babbo, and is very proud of his designation.

There is actually a chain of casual restaurants near us called Babbo Italian Eatery, which we frequent. A few years ago we had just finished eating there, and after most of us had dispersed from our seats, Tony and I remained at the table, me trying to contribute to the bill payment and him politely refusing. The waitress, however, returned to our table confused since Tony, as part of the bill payment, had included a $25 gift card for Amazon.com.

"I'm sorry, sir, I can't accept this," she said.

The gift card was a birthday present we had given Tony, and which was contained in an envelope labeled "Babbo."

---

[64] Not all Italians agree this is a legitimate term. For example, Uncle Paul, who, since discovering his brother-in-law wanted to be called Babbo, has taken to calling him "Bilbo," "Bo-Bo," and "Bozo the Grandfather Clown."

Babbo

Tony, without ever opening it, had wrongly assumed it was a gift card *to* Babbo. Once he realized his error, he turned on the charm.

"Oh my, goodness," he said to the waitress, "you're not going to believe this, ha, ha! *I* am Babbo. I completely forgot!"

She forced a smile.

He continued, "No, I am Babbo. You might think that *you're* Babbo, but no—*I* am Babbo! I thought this gift card was for Babbo but it was for Babbo, you know?"

The girl stood there with a look that said, "Can I just have your payment, please?"

"I don't even know if you know about Babbo ... do you? You work here, but I don't think you know about Babbo. It means, uh ... where did my pen go? Did you see my pen?"

"No, sir, I'm sorry, I did not," said the waitress.

"It means, uh ... you see that girl over there? THAT is why I am Babbo, not you. You know? That cute little girl over there, isn't she beautif—the pen was in my ear, ha!"

"Will that be all, sir?"

The Giver

Tony provides so much for the family, financially and otherwise. His gift to all of us is many-fold, perpetual, and impossible to repay, so he can be excused for lacking during moments set aside for specific gift giving. Besides, my mother-in-law, who undoubtedly noticed Tony's weakness very early on, is the brains and creative force behind all of the gifts any of us have ever received on behalf of them as a couple. In fact, if Tony is not physically present when you receive a gift bearing his name, and you thank him for it later, chances are he will have no idea what you are talking about.

Unfortunately for Anna, that means her husband's most glaring weakness really only manifests itself when he attempts to buy gifts for her. The legendary items he has purchased for Anna as gifts include a hot plate that read "Carrots," (Valentine's Day, '97) which was apparently part of an entire set of vegetable-related dishware that he either didn't notice or refused to buy, and a pair of compression socks. Compression socks, while not often described as romantic, do "guard against further progression of venous disorders such as edema, phlebitis, and thrombosis," according to Wikipedia. Sure, Tony could have gotten his wife flowers, but how is *that* going to help stave off thrombosis?

While wearing regular socks, we traveled back east for Christmas 2010, and on that Christmas Eve day, for a brief spell, Tony had disappeared.

At the time, no one really knew he was gone. Tony can sometimes be the type of man you only realize was gone when he reappears. The man is inherently sneaky. His very nature affords him the luxury of no one really knowing or caring what he is doing at any given moment. He could be inspecting the washing machine, in another room talking on his phone to a tenant who is screaming at him about noise coming from an upstairs apartment, at the gym, in the garage making sure the snow blower has enough gas or checking that his nine iron is still in his golf bag, in the middle of the street checking the sewers for reasons that will be revealed in time, taking a shower, installing a shower, playing ping-pong ... there are a limitless number of possibilities. The man's routine is *not having a routine*, so no one bats an eye when his whereabouts are uncertain.

Besides, it was Christmas Eve! How far away could he be? Certainly he was somewhere in the house, an assumption that became suspect when he reentered the house from the garage, carrying several plastic bags. Monica asked him where he'd been, but he mumbled something as he briskly walked upstairs.

The Giver

Christmas morning we all sat by the fire exchanging gifts. All of the attention centered on our daughter, then us "kids." When it was finally time for my in-laws to exchange Christmas presents, Tony excused himself to "go get something" upstairs. He arrived back downstairs holding plastic bags and saying under his breath to Anna, "Not sure if you wanted these wrapped ... "

He then began handing things to her out of a plastic bag like some sort of homeless Santa.

Anna's reaction to all of this progressed from slight confusion to utter bewilderment. She would give Tony, say, a scarf that he had seen in a store the previous month and claimed he really liked. In return she would get handed a Hershey bar.

"Okay, okay ... you know I like chocolate. Thank you, honey *(gives kiss).*"

Then she'd give Tony a case of his favorite wine. Her reward? A pair of youth mittens with rubber traction.

"Tony, what are ... alright. I mean, I'll have to return them for a different size. Are there unicorns on these? Okay, well. Your turn."

That Christmas morning everything culminated when my mother-in-law received an unwrapped box containing a plastic shoe rack. At this, Monica screamed, "Wait, you went to the drugstore, didn't you?"

Indeed, the previous day, Christmas Eve, he made a last-ditch effort to buy presents for his lovely wife at that beacon of feminine wont—CVS. The endless cacophony of unwrapped, pointless trash Anna was handed in honor of Christ's birth had us all clutching our sides with laughter. That included Tony himself, who had succumbed to the reality of his own questionable choices.

I couldn't help but picture Tony on line at the drugstore, hands full of junk, spotting more point-of-purchase junk that he easily talked himself into.

"A shoe rack, huh? She has shoes. That'll be perfect *(grabs it)*. I wonder if she has enough antacid … "

In Tony's defense, he typically balances out this lack of thoughtfulness with at least one very thoughtful gift. Sure, he may only do that after realizing he's made a huge mistake, but still. For example, he later gave her tickets to a Broadway show, to which Anna, if it was especially cold outside, could wear her unicorn mittens and bring her supersized bag of discount cough drops.

My brother-in-law Joe is a big hockey fan. In fact, he still plays hockey in various adult leagues.

Tony thought about his son's love for the sport when he noticed that the local hockey sporting goods store near his business in Brooklyn was closing down. He knew the owner, so he decided to go and see what he could get for his son at a discount.

"Here, take these skates," the owner said to Tony. "They're free."

Great, Tony figured—Joe would love these skates.

Tony arrived home and went so far as to box up the skates so he could present them to his son as an impromptu gift. A

The Giver

few days later, Joe and Jill invited Tony and Anna to their house for dinner. They accepted, and enjoyed a pleasant evening with their son and daughter-in-law. Just before leaving, Tony rushed out to the car to get the box. He handed it to his son and said, "Here. The hockey store near work is closing down, so I got you a little something. No big deal. Hopefully you can use them."

Joe thanked and hugged his dad, they said their goodbyes, and Joe went inside to open his gift.

The next day I received a text from Anthony, who was at Joe and Jill's house. It read:

> Dude. Dude. There is a hockey store in Brooklyn closing down so dad bought Joe skates. Let me know when you're ready for a picture of what he got.

I said I was ready.
Anthony replied:

> No, like you REALLY need to be ready. You should be at home when I send this, in a closed-off room with zero distractions. You are not ready at this moment.

When I arrived home that afternoon I texted Anthony back and told him I was ready.

I *thought* I was ready.

He sent the picture.

The Man in the Garlic Tuxedo

What made this all the more extraordinary was the fact that our daughter had recently started taking an ice skating class for kids three and up. Tony *knew* this. Yet when he saw the skates he was given by the store owner, he nevertheless insisted they should go to his son, thirty-three-year-old intramural hockey goalie.

We called Joe and told him to send us the skates since we could use them for his niece. He said, "I actually think they are too small for her," and then we heard him keel over into a helpless fit of laughter.

The Doctor

Tony grew up on naturopathic remedies because that was the only option. If spreading a combination of yeast and goat cheese on your upper thigh didn't get rid of the rash, then … well, you were out of luck.

Tony never entered willingly into America's open door of synthetic drugs. Remember, this is a man who owes his life to a chicken, so he can do without brompheniramine, thank you very much. He has remained committed to solving health problems naturally, when possible. For reference, it is always possible.

"Oh, you 'broke your arm'? Pfft. That's what the doctor *wants* you to think. Wait here, I'm gonna make you something …"

As I have come to learn, there are three essential ingredients to cure virtually anything, according to father-in-law,

The Man in the Garlic Tuxedo

MD. They are: garlic, honey, and lemon juice. Of these, the most important is garlic.

Obviously, garlic is a key ingredient in many Italian meals, and Tony is not shy about including it in whatever he is cooking. If he is cooking at our house and discovers that the garlic we have in our refrigerator is not fresh in that it was not purchased *that* day, he will become very agitated and will immediately drive to the store to get more. When he returns to the house and continues cooking, he will remind us twenty-five times that we should always have fresh garlic available, meaning we should purchase garlic every day of our lives.

Garlic has a well-deserved reputation for being pretty strong, but it does serve as a wonderful addition to certain meals. On its own, however, it is not very enjoyable to ingest. Most people, however, do not eat garlic straight, so this is not a typical concern.

Most people.

We were video chatting with my in-laws one evening after dinner, and my wife took it on herself to tell her father that I had a sore throat. He demanded I come closer to the computer.

"Mike, you have a sore throat?" Tony said.

"Yeah," I said. "Just started yesterday. No big deal."

"Listen, do you have garlic?"

"Uh, yeah, I think so."

"Is it fresh?"

"Umm, I mean, I'm not—"

"You should really always have fresh garlic."

Tony turned to Anna, who was sitting on the couch in the background.

The Doctor

"I keep telling them they should have fresh garlic."

"Stop bothering them!" Anna yelled to her husband.

"Listen," Tony said as he turned back to me, "go into the refrigerator and get three garlic cloves."

"Okay."

"You uh ... you gonna do it or what?"

"Oh, you want me to do it right *now*?"

"I don't know, I mean, if you want to feel better ... you called me."

I did not call him.

"No, no," I said, "okay, hold on ... "

I went into the fridge and took out some garlic and started peeling it. Tony watched me intently from the computer screen, giving me tips on how to better peel the garlic.

"Okay," Tony said, "now just put them all in your mouth and suck on them for a while."

"Umm, what? Are you serious?"

"I am very serious. Just suck on them ... trust me. I mean, you don't have to do it if you don't want to, but you asked for my advice, so ... "

I did not ask for his advice.

"Okay," I said, "here goes ... "

I popped the garlic cloves in my mouth and commenced sucking. Tony watched me suck on the garlic cloves.

"Can you feel it working?" Tony said.

"Umb, kind ofg ... "

"You'll feel better in no time."

After the video chat ended I immediately spit out the garlic and went upstairs to brush my teeth for six hours.

I am not certain that sucking on the garlic cloves soothed

my throat long term, but it definitely took my mind off having a sore throat for a few minutes. A sore throat, however, is one thing. Garlic is also useful for emergency health situations, although in such cases it should be combined with its trusty sidekicks, honey and lemon juice.

Monica was stung by a dang scorpion one day while at the kitchen counter. I was at the grocery store when it happened, so I couldn't even be there to avenge my wife's suffering by effeminately smashing the scorpion with a flip-flop. She handled that herself. She then called poison control before calling me, which was a great decision because poison control was calm and rational whereas I, when Monica did call me, abandoned my full shopping cart and deliriously rushed home while saying repeated Hail Marys.

Poison control informed Monica that she should be fine, although she would experience some pain. She should call back if her vision gets blurry, but other than that there wasn't much to do except deal with it. The pain of the venom had gone all the way up her arm and shoulder to her throat, but she endured it like a champ.

After things calmed down and we determined she was seeing straight, we had dinner and then called my in-laws to video chat to tell them what had happened. After *they* calmed down, my father-in-law expressed disappointment that poison control had not mentioned anything about garlic.

"Are they even trained?"

He gave Monica instructions on what to do. First, do we have fresh garlic?

The answer was no, but we said yes.

Do we have honey?

The Doctor

Yes.

Do we have lemons?

We did not have lemons.

For various reasons that included abandoning my shopping cart, I had already been to the grocery store three times in the past three hours. Monica did not want me to have to go out again, so she asked her dad if the lemons were really necessary. This was not a good idea.

One cannot make compromises on a Tony remedy. Would Michelangelo have sacrificed blue while painting the Sistine Chapel because he was too lazy to climb down the ladder and get some paint?

"Do you want to feel better or not?"

Fine. I said I would go to the store and get lemons. From the computer Tony yelled that I should get some fresh garlic, too.

I came back, and Tony walked his daughter through the garlic-honey-lemon recipe. The recipe is mixing them all together and then drinking it. I wasn't there when she was stung, but the look on my wife's face as she drank the concoction suggested that the pain of the remedy was much worse than that of the sting itself.

According to science,[65] the garlic, honey, and lemon juice combine their respective health molecules, travel through the bloodstream, locate the venom, and then punch it in the face. It's hard to say if that's exactly what happened, but Monica later claimed that the concoction did work to relieve the pain.

---

[65] A.k.a. Tony.

The Man in the Garlic Tuxedo

It also cured her sciatica and increased her heart rate by forty percent, for what it's worth.

Another satisfied patient.

The Patient

Tony had surgery to repair a hernia. He had waited to have the surgery so that he could run a half-marathon. Also, he ran the half-marathon with a ligament tear in his lower right leg. Anna was thrilled about all these things.

She was, however, non-sarcastically thrilled that the doctor had finally convinced her husband to utilize the provided anesthesia for the hernia surgery. You see, Tony, forever untrusting of people in general but doctors specifically, had decided he was going to stay awake for the surgery so that he could "see what the doctor was doing."

Had this been even remotely possible, it certainly would have involved helpful advice from the patient like "Do you really trust this brand of suture?" and "I'm not sure if that's how I'd approach the incision ... here, let me just ... where are the gloves?" It wasn't until the day of the surgery when my father-in-law finally listened to the graphic details of the

The Man in the Garlic Tuxedo

procedure and decided that maybe he didn't want to bear live witness or, you know, feel anything. One would think that being wide awake for tonsil removal by an unlicensed Italian naval officer would make him thankful for advances in anesthesiology, but I think it just gave him more resolve.

The surgery was a success despite Tony's unconsciousness and lack of verbal participation. He was given strict instructions to not do *anything* for at least two weeks except rest, to not lift anything weighing more than a remote control indefinitely, and to generally take it as easy as possible lest he damage the stitching on his lower abdomen.

The day after he returned home from the hospital there was a mild snowstorm in New Jersey. Still in the very early stages of his recovery, Tony thought it best to abide by the doctor's orders, and as a gesture of kindness and support, Anthony, Joe, and Jill came to the house to shovel the snow for him.

He was supposed to be lying on the couch the entire day, but Tony spent most of the time outside in his pajamas, micro-managing the snow-removal process. He gave Anthony detailed and redundant instructions on how to use the snow blower, although Anthony had used the snow blower many times and knew exactly what to do. It is likely that Anthony could have cut his time spent snow blowing by two hundred percent were he not burdened with having to listen to instructions on how to use the snow blower. Jill, according to Tony, was using the ice scraper incorrectly, and was possibly going to scratch the car. Joe was not shoveling the snow from the walkway in a manner that was pleasing. This situation was

The Patient

making everyone very happy, evidenced by the many texts Monica and I received as this was all taking place. Monica was also receiving texts from her father that included pictures of the action and complaints like "Look how your brother is snow blowing. It's going everywhere and he's going to kill the shrubs."

In Tony's defense, not only was he dealing with recovery and cabin fever, but he was also experiencing what he preferred to describe as bowel block. Here is a text he sent to Monica:

> Hi babes sorry didn't have a chance to answer your text I've been battling bowel block

The cautiousness with which he was forced to treat his abdominal stitches had presented a tenuous situation in which he was scared to use the bathroom. That fear then morphed into an inability to do so. This caused Tony, a man whose healthy and consistent diet meant you could set your watch to his bowel movements[66], much stress.

Luckily, the family was kept abreast of the ordeal via texts from Anna like "Pray for Dad, still no bowel movement. Will keep u informed," and "Dad thought he was going to go, but didn't. Almost there, stay tuned," and "DAD MOVED HIS BOWELS. SO RELIEVED. NO NEED TO SEND A CARD, JUST CALL WHEN YOU CAN."

After my father-in-law finally moved his bowels

---

[66] Not that I ever did. Okay maybe once.

post-hernia surgery, he was still staring down another week of prescribed bed rest. It had been about six days since the surgery when Anthony received a text alert while at work that read "Tony just completed a 2.35-mile workout!"

Before the half-marathon, Tony had set up his running app so that Anthony was sent alerts when he completed a run. This was done as a safety precaution because, as mentioned, Tony was running the half-marathon with torn ligaments plus a hernia, and if Anthony did not receive an alert after a certain time, maybe he should call an ambulance or something. (In this process, Tony also somehow set the app to send Twitter alerts when he completed a workout, which has been fantastic.)

Anthony was dumbfounded. He called his mom.

"Mom, I just a got a text alert which ... where is Dad? What is he doing?"

"Oh, you wanna know where you're fatha is?" Anna said. "Do ya'? Let me tell ya' where ya' fatha is ... he's out for A WALK. Yeah, believe that? Said he couldn't stay in the house anymore. He's wearing his workout headband. I don't know what to do with this man, Anthony. He's gonna have to go back to the hospital, God forbid. But at least he had the bowel movement. You know about that, right? Because I never heard from you."

One day after that incident my mother-in-law found herself searching the house for a man who was supposed to be on bed rest. She eventually found him ... in the crawl space of the basement, attempting to put away boxes of Christmas decorations, which was something he was explicitly told not to do since Anthony was coming over later to put the boxes

The Patient

away for them. Actually, he was no longer attempting to put away the boxes, but was instead wincing and holding his side.

"Anna," he said. "I just … I don't know, seems like where the stitches are might be a little swollen. I'm just hoping the stitches don't tear, you know? Not sure how this happened."

The Artist

The cat's already out of the bag regarding Tony's affinity for nude art, but it just so happens that this man of many talents is an artist himself.

The first time Monica led me into the great room of her family's home, I began admiring the paintings on the wall. I slowly began to realize that several of the works appeared to depict my wife and her brothers when they were young, and before I could get the question out she said, "My dad painted all these."

Listen, I know nothing about art. All I can say is that if Tony were a painter by trade I wouldn't be any less impressed. As far as I'm concerned, his work could pass for professional, and it's obvious when viewing his paintings that the blood of a creative artist runs through his veins.

The Man in the Garlic Tuxedo

Tony painted Matt golfing in Canada.

Many years ago he painted a portrait of JFK he saw on a magazine cover. By the way, replace JKF with Tony, and that is what I imagine my father-in-law envisioned the cover of this book would be. Minus the civil rights leaders yelling in

The Artist

the background. Unless we replaced them with Joe, Matt, and Anthony ... added some golf clubs ... I regret not doing this.

That goes exclusively for painting, however. His creative talent is not as obvious when looking at something Tony haphazardly drew for our daughter in an attempt to keep her entertained.

This picture keeps me up at night.

Surprisingly, considering his own eye for art, Tony often lacks the eye for other people's art.

During a stay in Arizona, my in-laws, their friends Tom

The Man in the Garlic Tuxedo

and Karen, and Anthony went out for dinner in a ritzy area of Scottsdale. After eating they went for a leisurely walk through town and passed an art gallery that was hosting a free exhibit. Outside, in front of the gallery, rested a sculpture that seemed to serve as the opposite of an invitation to come inside. It was of a naked woman flying, with birds embedded in her back, her body marked with holes. It probably meant something significant, but to the average person it looked like a sculpture of a naked, homeless, wannabe superhero—Bird Woman—who had been shot out of the sky by local police. As a result of this horrifying sculpture, nobody wanted to go inside. Except, that is, for Tony, the art critic.[67] So they all went inside.

Tony perused the locally produced art with keen interest. He walked slowly around the gallery, hand stroking his chin, examining the details of each work. My mother-in-law and Karen, turned off by the ludicrous prices and uppity vibe, left quickly and waited outside. Anthony and Tom remained, if only to monitor Tony and make sure he didn't break anything or cause a scene.

The artists responsible for each work stood nearby, eager to explain (and sell) their work to any interested passerby. As he strolled through, one particular painting piqued Tony's interest.

It rested on an easel, and below it sat the original photograph from which the work was obviously inspired. The two pieces, however, were very different. Comically different. It could just as well have been a third-grader's attempt to paint

---

[67] Few things reaffirm Tony's aspirations to do something more than when no one else wants to do it.

The Artist

her favorite picture, only if she had stopped in the middle of it to go watch TV. The painting, especially when set next to its inspiration, looked woefully incomplete. The artist standing proudly next to it was a woman who wore a long, ragged dress and had frizzled, red hair. She seemed to perfectly represent the stereotype of the whimsical, quirky artist. Of all the artwork and all the artists in the gallery, this is where Tony focused his attention. He had questions.

Tom and Anthony, who had previously and privately joked about the painting, saw Tony approach the artist and so they set their alert levels to high. Anthony stood at a distance while Tom bravely joined Tony, if only as a means to protect him from himself.

It did not work.

"So," the artist said to Tony, "I see this one caught your eye."

"Yeah, caught my eye," Tony said, "right, right. I was just looking around at the paintings and saw yours and uh ... I walked over."

"Okaaaay. So, have any questions for me?"

"Yes. When are you going to be finished with this?"

Tom bailed. ABORT. Anthony remained nearby, listening intently.

"I'm sorry?"

"This painting. When do you plan on finishing it?"

"Oh, it's finished. I mean, it's here, on display and all ... it's finished."

"Really? It's just that ... I don't know ... it looks like it could use more paint, maybe. I paint myself, so ... "

The Man in the Garlic Tuxedo

"Well, although I'm inspired by this original photo, I don't have a very literal perspective. I'm not sure how familiar you are with minimalism ... "

"Yeah, minimalism, right. There's definitely a lot of minimalism here."

"Are you interested in purchasing this piece?"

"*Purchasing*? WHAT? Pfft, no. I was just ... looking around. Besides, I was thinking, maybe, I don't know, that you might want to finish it before you sell it. I mean, it might be easier to sell it if it's finished, is a thought that I had, that I am just passing along. Maybe add some of those trees. It would be better if this had trees."

Speaking of trees, Tony was, according to Monica, a loyal Bob Ross disciple. Many a weekend morning her father could be seen standing at an easel in front of the television, following the instructions of the spectacularly afroed, soft-spoken host. Through this he mastered the painting of "happy little trees" and developed his artistic philosophy, which, we now know, rejects minimalism and doesn't mind some boobs. Although I don't think Bob Ross ever painted those.

The Safekeeper

If a person, especially a family member, entrusts something to Tony, there is absolutely no need to worry—he will never, *ever* let you down. He will never disclose your secret, never forget to do what you asked, never misplace what you gave to him. He is a walking vault if and when you need him to be.

If the ends justify the means, one need not be critical of exactly *how* Tony may go about being your safekeeper. His ways are known and understood only by him. Lest you become privy to some unnecessary anxiety, it is, in some cases, better to be ignorant to his process.

Take Matt, for example, who probably would have been better off not knowing what his father did with the engagement ring Matt had entrusted to Tony's care.

Matt was embarking on an event-filled weekend, closing on his first place in Washington, DC, Friday afternoon with

The Man in the Garlic Tuxedo

plans to propose to Maureen later that evening. Traveling south for both events were his loving parents, Tony and Anna. In fact, they were bringing the engagement ring, which Matt had ordered from New Jersey.[68]

Tony and Anna arrived at their hotel Thursday evening, settled in, and met Matt for dinner. Tony, who had made it his personal mission to be the ring's supreme caretaker, did not think it wise to leave the ring in the hotel safe. Instead, he kept it on his person.

Matt, understandably, was eager to see it up close for the first time, so he excitedly asked his father to show him the ring. Tony, while looking around ominously and skeptically at restaurant patrons as if any one of them could be a robber, spy, or former jilted boyfriend of Maureen, discreetly put his hand into the breast pocket of his sports jacket.

Matt waited anxiously, expecting his dad to unveil a smooth velvet bag, or a gold-lined ring case. Instead, Tony pulled out a crumpled up Dunkin' Donuts bag.

CRUNKLE CRUNKLE CRUNKLE. Tony's attempts to be discreet seemed quite silly considering the loud sound the bag was making in the relatively quiet restaurant. Matt was unsure what was happening.

"Dad, I asked to see the ring ... why are you opening garbage? Wait, please don't tell me that's where the ring—yep, that's where the ring is."

Amid the crumbs of a low-fat blueberry muffin rested Matt's ultimate sign of love for Maureen. He was almost too

---

[68] I, too, purchased my wife's engagement ring through a "connection" out of state. The connection was given to me by my wife, along with the ring type and specs. I really just had to order it.

The Safekeeper

distracted to appreciate the magnificence of the ring and what it stood for due to questions about its storage.

"Dad, it's just ... I mean ... *a Dunkin' Donuts bag?*"

It seemed to Matt, and to everybody on hearing this story, that Tony's commitment to keeping the ring *on* him was sufficient, and that he need not also keep it inside an old bag of food. Tony, however, an expert in street smarts, figured if anything happened to him in DC—a city as renowned for crime as politics—his assailant would never think to grab the crumpled up D&D bag in his breast pocket.[69]

Anyway, it didn't matter how the ring made it to DC, as long as it made it there. Besides, now it was Matt's ring to have and to hold.

Only it wasn't. Tony took the ring back from his son and returned it to the confines of the bag. CRUNKLE CRUNKLE CRUNKLE. Then he put the bag back into his jacket.

Matt, confused, said, "Dad, what a ... what are you doing? I think I can take it from here."

"Did you want me to take care of this?" Tony said. "You asked me to take care of this, so I am going to take care of this."

The dilemma of being able to trust Tony completely is that, unfortunately, he does not really trust you.

So they finished eating, walked around Dupont Circle, and stopped for some ice cream. At the end of the night, Matt again asked for the ring. Tony again denied this request. He was going to take it back to the hotel with him. It is as likely

---

[69] This is also the reason Tony does not carry money around in a big sack with a dollar sign on it. Instead he stores it in, again, an old Dunkin' Donuts bag.

The Man in the Garlic Tuxedo

Tony slept with the bag as it is that his pajama top has interior pockets, which is to say, very likely.

The next morning, Matt met up with his parents again. He asked his dad for the ring so he could leave it in a safe spot at his place before the closing. Tony did not think this was a good idea, and again refused. The ring was still in the Dunkin' Donuts bag. Tony brought it with him to the closing, safeguarding it further from thieves[70] as Matt signed endless amounts of paperwork.

After the closing, when they went back to Matt's official new place and celebrated by popping the cork on the champagne, Matt asked his dad again for the ring. He now needed it to, you know, PROPOSE TO MAUREEN. Reluctantly, Tony handed over the bag.

Just moments before Matt had planned to pop the question, he was finally given the ring he had entrusted his father to hold. As a result, the proposal went like this:

"And I love you, too. That's why … *(Matt gets down on one knee)* … *(CRUNKLE CRUNKLE CRUNKLE)*"

Okay, so not really. Matt *did* have enough time to present the ring in a more romantic way. To this day, however, Tony remains perturbed that Maureen has chosen to wear the ring on an open finger as opposed to somewhere just a bit more discreet.

---

[70] That was a subtle lawyer joke. Take THAT, lawyers.

The Man in the Garlic Tuxedo

There was, of course, the formality of Matt and Maureen actually getting married. We traveled back east for the festivities.

Monica and I walked out of the automatic doors of Newark Airport into a crisp, chilly fall midnight with an overtired two-year-old who was desperately excited to see her grandparents. We sensed something was wrong when we did not immediately spot their car illegally parked with its flashers on in a loading zone. When my in-laws' car finally pulled up at the curb, Matt was driving and my mother-in-law was sitting shotgun.

Where was Tony? It was unfathomable he wasn't there. He had never missed an opportunity to pick us up at the airport, especially when his granddaughter was in tow. It certainly wasn't the time of night that turned him off—he had gladly picked us up at more outlandish hours than this, and midnight is usually when he starts his day anyway. Our excitement at seeing our family was tempered by the burning question "Where is Dad?"

Tony was sick. Very sick, just two days before Matt and Maureen's wedding. Sick enough to not pick us up the airport. This was cause for concern. It takes a major bout of sickness for him to even *reveal* he's not feeling one hundred percent, much less have it affect his day-to-day life. He could be battling the bird flu and he would still go spinning at the gym in the morning to "work it out of his system."

When we arrived at the house, Tony did manage to drag himself downstairs to greet us. He looked terrible. He *smelled* terrible. He didn't even offer to make us something to eat, which seems silly to say but is probably the most accurate indication of how awful he was feeling. He was totally not himself. He took a shot of something and headed back upstairs, assuring us he'd feel better in the morning, although it seemed he was trying to convince himself.

"What had he taken a shot of and what was that smell?" were my questions at this time.

To combat his sickness, Tony had been getting a taste of his own oft-prescribed medicine—the garlic-honey-lemon elixir. He had taken things to the next level, however; the ratio of garlic to honey/lemon was at least ten-to-one, and he was taking shots of it whenever he passed through the kitchen. The process continued the next morning, and watching this happen was making the rest of us sick as well.

Meanwhile, as Tony was battling who-knows-what sickness, there was a problem with the tuxedos for the wedding party. The previous day, Matt and Anthony had gone to try

The Man in the Garlic Tuxedo

on their tuxes. They did not fit. It wouldn't just require a few alterations; it was more like "Whose tux is this? There is not an obese six-year-old boy in our wedding party with three legs." The store informed them that the earliest their new tuxes could arrive would be forty-eight hours, a.k.a. the morning we were all leaving for the Upstate New York wedding.

It had been twenty-four hours, and we were leaving the next morning. I had to go try on the tux that afternoon, as did cousin Sal and my father-in-law, who not surprisingly had waited until the last minute to do so. Based on the store's calculations, our tuxes would *have* to fit or else we'd be screwed.

Anthony drove us all to the tux rental store. Although Tony had proudly warned us beforehand that the car would reek of garlic as a result of his au natural battle to regain control of his immune system, it did little to prepare us for the actual smell of garlic that was emanating from his pores. It was suffocating. It wasn't like when something smells bad and you get used to it after a while. There was no relief. We couldn't roll the windows down because it was raining, and we couldn't even really joke about it with him because my father-in-law was in a foul mood due to his sickness.

He also appeared to be sleeping. His head was nestled against the passenger side window. We kept quiet, allowing him the peace to rest. We drove along in silence for about fifteen minutes, until that silence was broken by Tony who, with eyes closed shut, said, "Yeah, Dom. I need you to go see the tenant in 4E."

I assumed he was dreaming, and the thought that his dreams so exactly mirrored his day-to-day life made me laugh out loud. Anthony was equally stunned, as evidenced by the

The Man in the Garlic Tuxedo

look on his face as he turned to see what in the heck his dad was talking about. The confusion ceased when Dom the Supa responded from the speaker of Tony's cell phone.

Maybe not sleeping, but *definitely* with his eyes closed, Tony had either made a call from his cell phone, or received one on vibrate. The world of Brooklyn real estate and building management clearly does not stop simply because your son is getting married, and you are sick and oozing garlic and also sleeping.

After Tony hung up and we steadily approached our destination, I began silently praying from the back seat that the tuxes fit for the sake of both the wedding and the tuxedo rental store employees, who would have had their hands full with my *healthy* father-in-law. On this day, however, they would be facing my sick, frustrated, breathing-hot-garlic-fire father-in-law.

My prayers were not answered.[71]

Sometimes Tony goes in looking for a fight. This was one of those times. I knew he was already pissed off about how the store had mishandled Matt and Anthony's tux situation. Tony walked into the store ahead of us, wet from the rain, a scowl on his face, and leaving behind an odorous trail of garlic fumes that seemed almost visible, like the cloud left behind by Pepé Le Pew.

It was a battle before even entering the fitting room, as Tony, just by looking at the bagged tuxedo shoes prepared for him, expressed his disdain for them and claimed he'd be

---

[71] Well, I guess they were, actually, since I got a book out of it. God works in mysterious ways.

wearing his own. The workers pleaded with him that he should take the shoes just to be safe. One helpful employee reminded him that most brides prefer everyone in the wedding party to look the same, to which my father-in-law responded, "What bride? Pfft. I'm the father of the groom." He then kindly added, "I don't like your shoes."

My tux fit okay, thankfully. That wasn't really my concern though. The entire time I was getting changed I could hear Tony in the next stall complaining. At one point it sounded like he had summoned an employee *into* the fitting room with him in order to give him an earful, and it sounded like that because that is what happened. I could just picture this employee calling his friend after work.

"Yo, Chris. Yeah man, work was crazy. Dude smelling like mad garlic wouldn't shut up about how he hated our shoes. Got stuck in the dressing room with him. I need a drink."

Then it sounded like Tony was done with that employee, and not in a good way. He wanted somebody else. Was a manager involved? A manager was definitely involved.

When I emerged from my fitting room the first image I saw was that of Tony standing outside of his, hands on hips, rolling his eyes, with tuxedo pants that ended at his calves. The manager insisted it could be fixed with some minor tailoring and summoned the tailor over. Again an employee was forced to work in very close quarters with an angry man spewing garlic fumes.

The tailoring seemed to suffice. In retrospect I think Tony's sickness actually prevented this from becoming a much larger ordeal. There was no way he would have agreed to

The Man in the Garlic Tuxedo

those pants had he the energy to drag this fight out. *That's how sick he was.* Of course, that didn't mean he wasn't going to get in his two cents.

One of Tony's favorite things to do is complain to a third party about someone who is standing right there. The two of us went up to the front counter to pay for our tuxes. I was holding mine, and they were rolling his up on the wheeled, portable hanger.

"Look at that thing, Mike," he said to me, motioning to his bagged tuxedo ensemble. "I can't believe I'm paying money for that mess."

The manager who had assisted Tony in the process was the one ringing us up. I wasn't sure how to respond. Anthony and Sal made it a point to stay very far away[72] and I wished I were with them.

"What a joke this is," Tony added.

"I'm sorry, sir," the manager interjected. "Is there something you're still dissatisfied with?"

Tony did not answer. Instead he rolled his eyes and turned his back to the manager, an obvious implication that he wasn't going to waste another garlic breath on this man. The manager looked at me for some assurance that he should process the payment. I said, timidly, "I think it's okay."

Tony's health did not improve over the next two days, a shot to the heart of garlic's miraculous powers. Before we left for New York, we were seriously concerned about what role

---

[72] Besides avoiding a confrontational Tony, another reason they stayed far away was because Sal had farted in the front of the store. Neither here nor there, but we definitely did NOT make the Men's Wearhouse smell good that day.

if any he would play in his son's wedding festivities. Those of us close to him knew how terrible he was feeling. On the morning of our road trip, he *went to the doctor.* This was bad.

Before all this, weeks before the wedding, Tony had asked me if I wouldn't mind looking over a speech he had prepared for the wedding weekend. Tony had been tasked[73] with speaking at the rehearsal dinner, and this time, it seemed, he at least had the foresight to come prepared.

I was happy to look at his speech. Assisting him with the written word is pretty much the only way I can repay him for everything he does for me. So twice a year when he asks me to help him pen a formal letter to a tenant specifying that pythons are *not* an approved pet, I am thrilled to help. He told me he'd email me his first draft of the rehearsal dinner speech.

I had expected the speech to be him pouring out his love for his son on paper, reflecting on memories and the merciless speed with which time moves, and expressing his yearning for a future of hopes and dreams fulfilled. I would attempt to organize those thoughts and feelings into a cohesive finished product. He sent an email with instructions for me look it over, provide my thoughts, etc.

I opened the attachment. It looked like a blank document until I saw the smidge in the upper left-hand corner. This is the version of the speech he sent:

"I knew Maureen before I even met her because I always

---

[73] By himself.

dreamed my son would find someone like her. Now I am so happy to have another daughter. You don't need a GPS to find love."

I was taken aback by its brevity, but I figured that maybe Tony was turning over a new leaf and was going to keep it simple. Maybe Anna had finally gotten to him. In my response I told him I liked how it was short and sweet, but uh ... I wasn't quite sure what to make of the last line.

I figured Tony had been inspired along the way by the truth that, no—contrary to popular belief, you *don't* need a GPS to find love, and he was going to include that sentiment in his speech no matter what, meshing yet again his love for his children and technology. I wondered if the subject of a GPS device could be brought up earlier in the speech so as to bring everything around for the ending metaphor. Possibly he had once witnessed Matt and Maureen argue over directions, and that argument revealed their true love for each other? Maybe? No? No.

In our correspondence it was also revealed that what he had sent was just "a guide," and he thanked me for my input. He was pretty much going to wing it again anyway, so ... yeah. My services were largely unnecessary.

The morning of the rehearsal dinner, as we furiously packed several cars to make the hour-long trip up north, Tony returned from his visit to the doctor. He looked pale and awful, but assured us he was okay. We asked him what the doctor said, and he responded in grunts, something along the lines of "she doesn't know what she's talking about," as he went upstairs to get his bags.

When we reached the hotel, Tony went right to his room

The Man in the Garlic Tuxedo

for a nap to rest for the rehearsal dinner. He awoke a couple hours later feeling no better than before, but duty called. No time for excuses. His son was getting married, and he needed to give a speech.

In the lobby of the hotel and on the bus ride to the restaurant, Tony acted the part, giving no indication of his struggles and embracing his role as father of the groom. He smiled, laughed, and engaged in conversation. We knew it was killing him.

We all filed into the restaurant, grabbed our drinks of choice, and began socializing. When the food came out, that was Tony's cue. He would speak as everyone was just starting to eat.

Anna was simply hoping he'd be able to stand upright for the speech, but the whole day I kept wondering: "Is he going to use the GPS line?"

He got up to speak. He thanked Maureen's parents. He thanked everybody for being there. He talked about Matt as a young boy, and how he can't believe the way time passes.

He then turned to Maureen's father and said, "And you may not know this, but I've known Maureen longer than *you*!"

The crowd was intrigued.

"Because I am older than you, and I have dreamed about her my whole life."

The crowd was slightly confused.

"Because I have dreamed about my son finding a girl like her."

The crowd said, "Awwwwww."

Then he went on about some things that were definitely

not contained in his first draft, and there were a few awkward pauses as he tried to remember the details of whatever he was talking about. I could tell that Anna, sitting next to him, was tapping him on the leg to wrap it up.[74] This time he heeded her advice. That, or he was about to pass out. He raised his glass.

I was relieved but also a bit disappointed. I knew the line had no place in the speech, especially since he had obviously not included a technology-related anecdote that would have brought it full circle. I was, however, sort of looking forward to it for those very reasons. I had even pulled Matt aside earlier and warned him that it may go down and to be prepared if his love for Maureen was compared to a smartphone app. Matt then told everyone else at our table, and during the entire speech we were all on the edges of our seats with anticipation. Now I looked like a false prophet. Somewhat crestfallen, I raised my glass.

He toasted, "To Matt and Maureen … you don't need a GPS to find love."

My wife is considerably less sensitive than, say, my sister Jill. If you insult Monica, she is more apt to insult you back than to wallow in sadness. This is probably the result of being a lifetime victim of accidentally offensive Tony comments and being forced to defend herself. However, sometimes the setting of Tony's comment—not its recipient—is what makes it memorably offensive.

---

[74] My mother-in-law's face during any Tony speech is a splendid mix of a fake smile and "what is he going to say or do?" anxiety.

The Man in the Garlic Tuxedo

It was the day of the wedding, and everyone was immersed in the rush of readying themselves. As he is wont to do, my father-in-law was the last of the men to be ready, as he had decided to squeeze in a workout at the hotel gym despite his illness.

Or because of it. Tony had awoken that day feeling just slightly better than the previous day, but still not close to what could be considered feeling well. Using what little energy he had, he dragged himself down to the exercise room with plans to sweat out some of the sickness before the wedding. So, while the rest of us were frantically trying to piece together our complicated tuxedo parts, he was on an exercise ball performing a routine he had seen on Dr. Oz.

The guys were ready to head down to the lobby, but Tony wasn't there, so I went to his room to check on his progress. I walked into a familiar scene, a room filled with tension.

My mother-in-law was left frustrated yet again by the tardiness caused by her husband's curious daily decisions, and any sympathy she may have had for his tenuous health had obviously dissipated. Tony was standing there, half dressed, with a handful of buttons that came with his tuxedo. He had a look that said I have all these buttons, but I don't know what to do with these buttons. I quickly deduced that Anna had given up on assisting him, and that Tony was going to stand there holding the buttons until someone helped him with the buttons. It seemed I had walked in at a very opportune time for Matt and Maureen, whose plan it was to get married that day at a predetermined time and location.

I installed various buttons on Tony's wardrobe as he stood there saying, "I don't know … with these buttons."

It was then Monica stormed in, obviously sharing our

collective concerns. "What the hell is going on? We have a wedding to go to!" She then began the more abstract task of tending emotionally to her frustrated mother.

After helping her mom, Monica was then tasked by her father with fixing his boutonniere. The man who learned carpentry at age five had been befuddled by several buttons and a safety pin.

Now my wife and I were both working in close physical proximity to Tony, which gave us a chance to breathe in the fresh smell of recently ingested garlic, and gave *him* a chance to get a good look at us.

Apparently, I did not notice that Monica had one or two small acne spots on her face that were covered up with makeup. But nothing gets past Tony. After looking at his daughter, he took it on himself to say, "Oh, I uh, see you got some poppers there on your face."

Under calmer circumstances, the ongoing fact that he calls zits "poppers" would have provided enough hilarity to mask the offensiveness of that statement. These were not calmer circumstances. Monica's reply—"WHAT?!"—was enough to alert Tony that he had made a poor verbal decision, a reality he responded to by shrugging and repeating under his breath, "I don't know, it's just some poppers, no big deal."

Anna, sensing the impending explosion, said, "LET'S GO," and we left the room. I tossed the unused buttons.

I later learned that it was not only Tony's lateness that had accounted for the tension between him and my mother-in-law, but also the fact that he had commented to his wife that her dress—the beautiful dress she was wearing for her son's wedding—"didn't fit so great."[75] This is something he had said to her five minutes after we were scheduled to meet in the lobby.

Herein lies the paradox: Tony was right. Anna had sensed the dress wasn't fitting well, but had ultimately decided to just go with it, unsure of what else to do. She could have gone with it, and it wouldn't have looked as great as it ultimately did, and no one would have said a peep to her about it because no one is like my father-in-law. So, when my wife had walked in the room, they made an adjustment to the dress, and it worked.

That, in a nutshell, is Tony. He will tell you the last thing you want to hear at the most inopportune time, and more often than not he will be right.

It is quite maddening for us regular folk.

Anna would mend her dress, and she and Tony would mend their fences, and the wedding was beautiful. Now it was time to party.

The wedding reception provided another social occasion during which Tony would try to overcome his sickness for the greater good. He would succeed.

Who knows, maybe he did sweat it out at the gym. Or maybe his sheer resolve to have fun and not adversely affect the festivities carried him through. Whatever the case, he appeared to be his normal self. During the reception, which

---

[75] It should be noted, if it's not already apparent, that Tony often combats sickness and bad moods with even more brutal honesty than usual.

The Man in the Garlic Tuxedo

featured no silly props, he was witnessed dancing happily with some sort of object on his head. That object was called a mute, which is something trumpet players use to adjust the sound of their instruments. It looks like a combination of a plunger and a dunce cap. Somehow, Tony had acquired this mute from the wedding band's trumpet player:

"HEY, CAN I BORROW THIS?"

"ACTUALLY I NEED IT FOR MY INSTRUMENT."

"I WAS GOING TO WEAR IT ON MY HEAD. I AM THE FATHER OF THE GROOM."

"OH, OKAY, HERE."

Months later the pictures from the wedding arrived, and one stood out from all the rest. It featured neither Matt nor Maureen. It was of Tony on his knees in front of the wedding band—which had just ended its set for the night—his finger in the air begging for *one more song*. It was past midnight when that picture was taken.

I do not think one thing better exemplifies the man as a whole than Tony's performance as "the man in the garlic tuxedo." His stubbornness, his resolve, his relentless pursuit of joy, his way with words, his selflessness, his commitment to his family, and most importantly, an unwavering trust in naturopathic, garlic-based remedies.

He was as sick as a person could be who is not bedridden, but like hell was he going to let that stop him from enjoying his son's wedding, and like hell was he going to elicit any sympathy from strangers by cluing them in on his physical battle. Instead, he danced the night away, with a weird thing on his head, and then refused to leave.

He danced in his own shoes.

The Greatest Communicator

Text from Anthony to me:

> I called dad trying to tell him I'm at the North side curb for pickup at the airport and he got into a 3 minute spiel about how to get from the plane to the baggage claim. I was like dad I dunno what you're even talking about but just meet at the North curb
> It's almost as if he assumes you are an alien suddenly dropped onto the planet for the first time and have no clue what anything is or means

Monica and I were not there for the infamous "Captain Speech." It is one of our few regrets about moving to Arizona.

In the middle of a holiday family dinner, my father-in-law stood up at the table. He just wanted to say a few words.

The Man in the Garlic Tuxedo

To this day no one is quite sure what inspired Tony to speak. Not that it was unusual whatsoever for him give an unexpected, freestyle speech, but this one was different. This one was completely out of nowhere. This one was a metaphor. It began:

"This family is a ship, and every ship has a captain. I AM the captain of this ship."

With Tony, there is a time for joking and a time to be serious. Even the most socially unaware person can read my father-in-law's mood to determine whether or not it's a good time to joke with him. This was not the time to joke with him. This meant it was inappropriate and highly risky to laugh during this speech, which was extremely difficult since my father-in-law was bestowing on himself the honor of captain of the family ship. Oh, also:

"The ship is going down."

To what, exactly, he was referring remains a mystery. Who at that very table was responsible for causing a leak in the family ship? Joe? Aunt Liz? My mother-in-law? Who released the anchor on the deck? Certainly it couldn't have been my wife and me, since there is no water in Arizona.

"But I will save the ship!"

Whew!

"I just want to let you know that I love you all, even though you're not kids anymore. You're all so beautiful."

I forget where Monica and I were as this speech was taking place, but I remember our phones were *blowing up* with texts. Anthony and all of my wife's cousins were texting us—phones underneath the table as the speech was happening—with comments like "Omg you CANNOT believe what is happening

The Greatest Communicator

right now!" and "Dad ... captain speech ... no words ... will call asap."

Uncle Paul bravely attempted to interject by making a lighthearted comment that would hopefully serve to end the awkwardness. It did not work. Tony either did not take the hint or ignored it. Uncle Paul, mere deck hand, returned to his original position of silence, relegated to hearing more from his brother-in-law and captain.

It went on, and on, and on. Possibly overcome with nostalgia, Tony was harkening back to his merchant marine days and reinventing himself as family ship captain. Who knows. Anthony would later sum up the awkwardness by saying that if he had ever in his entire life been granted the ability to turn invisible and remove himself from a situation, the "Captain Speech" would have been it. Hands down.

Whatever happened that day, all I know is this: The ship *was* saved.

I know this because we're still sailing along.

Aye, aye.

I walked into Barbeque World to pick up a grill cover for my father-in-law who, after an extended stay at his Arizona home, had returned to New Jersey. Before he left, he had ordered a cover for his backyard grill to, quite ironically, protect it from the extreme heat. He had received word that the grill cover had arrived, and I agreed to go pick it up. The previous night Anna had called Monica to remind her to remind *me* about getting the grill cover, and earlier in the day Tony had texted me to confirm I would, in fact, be getting the grill cover. At this point I was well aware of—albeit a bit confused by—the importance of properly obtaining this grill cover.

"Hi, can I help you with something?" asked Jim from Barbeque World.

"Yeah, hi," I said. "I need to pick up a grill cover for my father-in-law. He was here last week and put one on order to be picked up."

"Oh. Uh, okay. What's the name?"

"Tony ... "

Jim briefly checked a binder underneath the register and found nothing. He walked into a room in the back of the store and then reemerged holding nothing. I felt sorry for him immediately, and also for myself.

"Ummm, do you know who he spoke with?" Jim asked. "We usually don't hold things like that for people. What probably happened is that the cover he wanted came in. We just got a bunch of grill covers in the other day."

"I'm not really sure who he spoke with," I said.

"Do you know which cover he wanted?"

"No, I thought it was here for pick up. He's out of town. Let me call him."

I called one of Tony's thirteen phones. It rang. And rang. Then the phone picked up. There were some random noises.

"Hello?" said Tony.

"Hey, Dad," I said.

"Mikey! Baby! Oh boy, we gotta get that little girl of yours over here for some dinner and ... "

His voice trailed off and I heard some fumbling around. I

The Greatest Communicator

assumed he was on the Outerbridge Crossing with a coffee in one hand, the phone on his shoulder, a different phone in the other hand with which he was cursing at Comcast cable, and driving with his knees.

"And uh, stuff her full of food," he continued, "and … uh … "

Silence.

"Dad?"

"Yeah … what a, what are you doing?"

"Hey, yeah, I'm actually at the barbeque place right now and I just—"

"What barbeque place are you at?"

"Barbeque World, on Jackson and 75th."

"The one on uh, Jackson and … 75th Avenue?"

"Yes. The one you told me to go to."

"Barbeque World?"

"Yes."

"What place are you at? On 75th?"

"Yes. Dad, so uh, I asked for your grill cover and they don't have anything here waiting for you, and the guy said—"

"Let me talk to the guy."

"Oh. Ummm, actually, do you remember who you spoke with because—"

"Put the guy on the phone."

I valiantly attempted to not put Jim in the position of talking to my father-in-law over the phone, to no avail.

"Well there's a couple guys here," I said, "so if you remember who you spoke with, maybe one of them—"

"Maybe you can uh, put the guy on the phone and I can talk to him."

The Man in the Garlic Tuxedo

I handed the phone to Jim, giving him a sheepish, "Good luck—this one's outta my hands now" half-smile. He looked at me, confused.

"Uh, hello?" Jim said. "Yes ... uh huh ... Barbeque World ... ummm, on 75th Avenue and Jackson Road ... yes ... Barbeque World ... okay ... yeah."

Jim walked to the back room with my phone. I aimlessly walked around the store pretending to look at grills. Then I moved toward the back of the store to find out what was going on.

"Okay, does your grill have red buttons?" I heard Jim ask Tony. "Like, red buttons for igniting? ... Yes, your grill ... But does it have red buttons? ... Okay ... Yes ... Barbeque World ... uh huh."

In an attempt to throw Jim a bone, I whispered loudly that the grill has three black burner knobs. He nodded at me and gave me a grateful thumbs up.

"Alright," Jim said, "well we only have two covers for that kind of grill, so let me ask you this ... Yep ... Lemme just ... Uh huh ... Okay, is your grill flat on top, or does it angle upward? ... Yes, the top of the grill ... I mean, is it flat on top, or does it like, angle upward? ... Okay, yeah ... I mean, if you put something on top of your grill, will it fall off?"

I whispered loudly to Jim that the grill is flat on top. He nodded.

"Okay," Jim said, "so no ... yeah ... okay, I know what grill cover you need, so I'm just going to ... yeah ... okay ... okay ... okay."

Jim desperately tried to hand the phone back to me, but

The Greatest Communicator

each time he was about to hand it to me he brought it back to his ear to say "okay" and appease Tony, who was still talking. Finally, Jim handed me the phone and walked away briskly. When I placed it to my ear Tony was still talking.

"Dad-Dad-DAD," I said, interrupting him. "Hey, it's me."

"Mike? WHAT?" Tony said, annoyed. "I wasn't finished talking to him. I don't know, I just ... I wasn't finished talking to him. Mike?"

"Yes. It's me."

Jim walked past me back toward the register holding a box that contained the grill cover.

"Mike, listen," Tony said, "what does the grill cover look like?"

"I don't know, Dad," I said. "It's in a box."

"Oh. Is the box flat?"

"Is the box *flat*? Uh, yeah, I mean, it's not one of those ... round boxes."

"What color is the grill cover?"

"What color is it? I don't know. It's in a box."

Jim overheard me and whispered to me that the grill cover was black. Jim and I were going to get each other through this, somehow.

"It's black, Dad," I said to Tony. "He said it was black."

"It's black? Okay, good. It should be black. It's black?"

I noticed Jim scan the box and the price load to the register.

"And it's $39.95," I said to Tony.

"WHAT?" Tony said. "Noooooo, $39.95? No. Tell him he's gotta do better than that."

"Uh, really?"

The Man in the Garlic Tuxedo

"Can you see if he can do better than that?"

"Ummm, do you want me to negotiate for the grill cover?"

"Let me talk to him."

I had given up. I handed the phone back to Jim, who winced.

"Hello?" Jim said. "Uh, okay ... uh huh ... ummm ... well, I guess I could give you the fireman's discount ... ten percent off? ... yeah? ... okay ... okay."

Jim did the thing again where he tried to hand the phone back to me but couldn't. "I'm just gonna," Jim said, "hand the phone back now ... to him."

I took the phone, unsure whether or not my father-in-law just told Jim that he was a firefighter.

"Dad?" I said.

"Yeah, Mike," Tony said. "I got the discount."

"I know."

"It's gonna be ten percent. That's okay, for now."

I was unsure whether this meant Tony would attempt to get additional discounts on his return to Arizona, but did not doubt it.

"Okay," Tony said, "so uh, I hope that the grill cover fits because if it doesn't, I'm sorry, but I'm gonna need you to return it. Because, ya know, it uh, it needs to fit on the grill."

"No problem," I said. "I'll test it out this weekend, probably tomorrow."

"It's just because, it needs to fit."

"Yes. I'll try it tomorrow."

"Maybe you can try it tomorrow."

"Yes. That's a good idea."

The Greatest Communicator

"Okay, is that it?"
"Yep, I think that's it."

Text from me to Anthony:

> We're at The Good Egg for breakfast, dad orders crab omelette, gets it, says, "What? It tastes like there's fish in here ... "

The following is an email Tony sent to Monica from the airplane on a flight back to New Jersey.

> Hi Babes,
> We are schedule to arrive at Newark 45 minutes early, we left at 4pm
> I and mom were at Fox bar having some late lunch and I had a beer when we realized the passengers were already boarding the plane was, mom was going to the bathroom at 20 to 4pm, and she screamed hey they are boarding so she left and got on the plane
> i didn't know if she had gone to the ladies room or not, so I was going to wait for her when they called me and said she was trying to leave without me, he guy started laughing
> I picked up behind her getting on on the plane, then she went to the bathroom and when the guy saw me he said " she really left you ?"

The Man in the Garlic Tuxedo

Boy oh boy she wasn't going to let go of the "A boarding" anyway its quite snowy below us, will talk soon
Love Dad

    I have seen samples of Tony's professional correspondence, and it is consistently well put together. My theory is that during any email or text back-and-forth with his family, he tends to be lax from his duties as a professional, which is fine. We certainly don't require perfect grammar, but these emails and texts often make for quite the confusing literary journey. The inclusion of random details is also perplexing. I don't know if him having a beer is relevant to the overall story.[76] Should I remember that for later? Not sure. I think the main point is that my mother-in-law was "going to the bathroom," a turn of phrase I'm sure she appreciates very much. My mother-in-law goes to the bathroom many times in this brief story.

    I similarly enjoy the random appearance of "the guy," a.k.a. "he guy," who I'm not sure was properly introduced.

    The first time Monica showed me this email I read it approximately fifteen times, studying it intently as if trying to decode an ancient Arabic text that could possibly be a hidden gospel. Eventually my head physically fell off of my body and rolled on the floor into the living room. I picked it up, put it back on, and took a three-day nap.

---

[76] Had he mentioned he drank *six* beers, however, then this email would make complete sense.

The Greatest Communicator

Text from Anthony to me:

> On the plane dad got the Jewish man next to him to say the travel prayer with him and make the sign of the cross LOL

My brother-in-law Joe is the goalie for an adult men's hockey league team, the Inferno, that features guys who range in age from their early twenties to mid-fifties. One season Joe's hockey team made it all the way to the championship game. Tony and Anna decided to go and cheer on their son.

Well, Anna *went*, but not necessarily to cheer. Actually, she didn't watch any of the game, overcome with the raw emotion a mother experiences when her oldest son is attempting to withstand the rigors of adult league hockey on such a large stage.[77] According to my sister Jill, also in attendance to support her loving goalie/husband, Anna spent the first period covering her eyes and muttering, "I can't watch, I can't watch," and by the second period had left the stands and was nowhere to be found. Too bad, because besides the game itself, she missed the inspiring words of her husband, who certainly *did* show up to cheer.

After falling behind in the first period, Joe's team mounted a comeback in the second. This greatly excited the fans in attendance, and by that I mean one fan in particular. It's unknown if Joe's hockey team began playing better because of or

---

[77] That stage being The Arenas in Woodbridge, New Jersey, near the Woodbridge Mall.

despite the curious cheers coming from a man in the stands. Cheers that included:

"Go, yeah!"

"Shoot the puck, shoot it NOW!"

"Go get 'em, Inferno, with hockey!"

"You can do it, I'm here for you!"

"NOW, GET HIM!"

"If you score I'll take you all to dinner!"

"Bad shot! What was THAT?"

"Put your best foot forward!"

"Doing great, but you can do better!"

"Go! Do it!"

"If I could I'd go sit behind the bench and help coach!"

"GO FOR THE GOAL!"

Amused by the tenacity and fervor of the goalie's dad, the wives/kids/moms/dads/fans of Joe's team smiled, laughed, and egged Tony on as he continued his cheering assault. The fans of the other team, however, shot eye rolls and glances of disgust from across the stands throughout the game. A middle finger or two may have been involved, although this has not been confirmed. These polar opposite reactions to his cheering each served, in their own unique ways, as motivation for Tony to cheer more fervently, which he did.

Unfortunately, the early deficit proved too much for Joe's team to overcome, and they ended up losing the championship game. As his tired, frustrated, and disappointed team entered the locker room after the game, one of Joe's teammates interrupted the silence by yelling, "Yo, alright—who the hell was that Spanish guy yelling at us from the stands the whole game?"

The Greatest Communicator

Joe said, "Actually, that was my dad. And he's Italian."

His teammate apologized profusely, and Joe readily accepted since he would have assuredly been asking the same question if the skate were on the other foot. After reassuring him further that it was quite alright to have questioned the identity of the madman in the stands, Joe's teammate asked him, "So ... was he really going to buy us dinner?"

"Oh yeah, he definitely would have taken us to dinner," Joe said. "If you guys would have SCORED."

The team laughed, and the ice was proverbially broken.

Inferno is Italian for "hell," and that's what Tony gave 'em. The Inferno's opponent, that is. But also the Inferno.

Mostly the Inferno.

Text from Anthony to me:

> Dad watching The Masters with me. Me: Guys look at this stupid shirt this guy behind Jason Day is wearing. Dad: I KNOW THIS GUY that's Nick he did my windows on 66th street I'm gonna call him!

How this probably played out:
"Nick! It's Tony!"
"Tony who?"
"*Tony*, from 66th Street!"
"Oh, uh ... hey."
"I saw you on TV!"
"What? When, where? On the news? You didn't tell anyone, did you?"

The Man in the Garlic Tuxedo

"No, at The Masters! You were standing behind golfer Jason Day, wearing a weird-looking shirt."

"Is this a joke? Listen, Tony, I'm busy. You want your windows washed or what?"

Tony does not understand that with Siri—the female-voiced audio helper on late model iPhones—one must be direct and to the point with a question. He speaks to her as he would a regular human, which is to say with words that often don't make sense. His utter lack of success in utilizing Siri to access information makes it a wonder he continues to try. Every time I have witnessed him attempt to interact with Siri, I have thought to myself, even *I* don't understand that question, and I am a person. There are countless examples of this. Here is one.

The scene is this: We're all sitting on the couch watching the Australian Open on TV. Juan Martín del Potro, a number six seed, is facing unranked Jérémy Chardy and losing. Tony is rooting for del Potro for reasons that are not apparent or important. In fact, even he's not sure why. To find out more about the man for whom he is rooting, Tony takes out his phone to access Siri.

"Hey a, Sirious, how are you? Listen ... who's Potro?"

Tony calls Siri "Sirious." It's part of the S-disease, yes, but it also makes us laugh, so now I think he does it on purpose for the goof. Of course, this does not help whatsoever in the effort of getting information. Also, because of Tony's strong Italian accent, it's imperative he annunciate with Siri, which he does not do. In an effort to be casual about the whole thing, like "This is what the kids are doing, no big deal," he is barely audible when he asks the question. A little thing like greeting Siri at the outset—unnecessary, she knows who she is, and also he calls her the wrong name—throws a monkey wrench into the whole endeavor. He is done before he even starts. Not only does he not provide any background or preface to his question—i.e., "tennis player"—he doesn't even use *the entire last name*. Saying the entire last name is useful if you're trying to search for someone solely by last name. Staying with the tennis theme, it would be like me trying to search for Billie Jean King by asking, "Who is King?" Of all the questions he has asked Siri, and there have been some doozies, this might be the one that was most doomed from the start.

"I'm sorry, I do not understand the question," said Siri.

Tony laughed, humored by Siri's idiocy.

"Sirious ... Who is Potro?"

"Hold on, let me check. Searching for 'Who is Papi?' Is that correct?"[3]

"Ha, Papi! Did you guys hear that? She's gonna search for Papi. Siri—"

"I'm sorry, I do not understand the question."

"My goodness, she doesn't let you talk. Sirious, listen. Who is—"

"Would you like me to search the Web for 'Who is Papi?'"

"Will you stop it?" Anna said. "We're trying to watch the game!"

"Ha, 'game.' Anthony, she called it a game. Anna, it's a *match*, not a game."

"Searching for 'Anna match game,'" Siri said. "Is that correct?"

The Man in the Garlic Tuxedo

"This is not to be believed," Tony said. "Sirious, pay attention. Who is Potro?"

"Dad," Anthony said, "she's not gonna get that. You have to give her more information."

"Searching for 'Who is Ponyo?'" Siri said. "Is that correct?"

"Dad," Anthony said, "honestly, let me look him up on my phone. It'll take two seconds."

"What?" Tony said. "Who is Ponyo? Pfft."

"Okay," Siri said. "I'll search the Web for 'Who is Ponyo' ... " End scene.

By the way, *Ponyo* is a Japanese animated fantasy film that Disney released in America in 2009.

As if accessing Siri for information and failing terribly and consistently weren't enough, Tony has also tried to use Siri to send texts while driving. He sent the following text to his niece after she was accepted for an important internship:

> Congratulations sweetheart I am in the car with Ann Anna driving to drop TV and Antles good news I want to wish you luck series is assisting me with this text

"Ann Anna" = Aunt Anna
"drop TV" = drop (off) Tibby (the dog)
"and Antles" = at Aunt Liz('s)
"series" = Siri (although he undoubtedly said "series" or "Sirious")

This text doesn't make much sense even post-translation:

The Greatest Communicator

"Congratulations on your internship. I am dropping the dog off at Aunt Liz's house."[78]

I think my favorite part of this text, however, is the fact he felt compelled to acknowledge that he utilized Siri to send it, as if the text itself should be a source of pride.

It's tough not having family around most of the time, but thankfully we live in an age where it can be made to feel like family is present even when they are thousands of miles away. This is especially important for our daughter, who is always aching to see all four of her grandparents, and is able to do so thanks to the wonders of modern technology.

FaceTime is a built-in feature on the iPhone whereby one can video chat with a fellow iPhone user. It's possible we use this feature more frequently than the regular ol' phone audio because our daughter's grandparents would prefer to see her rather than only hear her, and vice versa. They couldn't care less about us, honestly. I don't even make an appearance in the majority of our FaceTime sessions, spending most of them in the background washing dishes.

These calls offer varying degrees of success, and by that I mean they are almost always unsuccessful. FaceTime calls with my parents freeze constantly. They have an old router that they

---

[78] Tony has a knack for responding to text messages by simply telling you what is doing at the moment. Monica recently sent him a picture of our girls in their bathing suits with the following note: "Heading to the pool. Wish you were here!" His response? "In the middle of tying a big table on my car roof."

acknowledge is at fault, yet they lack confidence in their ability to set up a new router, and so the beat goes on. When we FaceTime freeze with my parents, we can quickly come to a mutual decision that it isn't working and end the call.

It's not so easy with my in-laws, and they *also* have a faulty router that makes freezing the norm. The difference is that Tony refuses to acknowledge his router is to blame, proving only his stubbornness can get in the way of his love for technology. Even tech-savvy Anthony has urged his dad to buy a new router, but Tony remains convinced everyone else's device is the problem. So, the beat goes on. Monica actually started saving the pictures of the awful freeze-frame shots of her mother that happen when the call freezes, creating a collage entitled "Nanny's Expressions." Regardless of how well it's not going, my in-laws always want to try again, and their router will always fail ... again.

That's the thing with FaceTime—you need to be on an Internet connection to use it. Or so we thought one day as we FaceTime-called my in-laws to see if they were home to speak with their precious little one. They were driving home at the time, but Anna decided to pick up the call anyway.

Apparently, the latest iOS iPhone update that both Monica and Tony had recently installed allowed for FaceTime on 3G, and wouldn't ya' know it—it worked. The phone sat on our kitchen table in front of our daughter as this ensued:

"AHHHHHH!" Anna screamed. "IT WORKED! WE'RE DRIVING! Hi, baby girl! We're driving! Can you believe this?"

"HA, HA, HA!" Tony said. "It's a miracle! How's my baby girl doing? It's Baaaaabooooo! We're driiiiiviiiiing ... do you see us driving, honey? We seeeeeee youuuuuuu! We're in the car. How is this happening?"

Tony started talking to Anna.

"Hey, show her the car. She wants to see the inside of the car."

"Tony," Anna said, "STOP! It's a red light. I can't believe this ... how is my girl? Did you have a good day at school today?"

Our daughter said, "I—"

"HOW'S MY GIRL?" Tony interrupted. "Do you see us driving, honey? I don't understand how this is happening. Mike—how is this happening? We are driving."

From the kitchen sink I said, "I don't know, Da—"

"Tony," Anna said, "you missed the turn! Are you even paying attention? Wait, hold on, honey ... "

Anna started talking to Tony.

"Did you give him the papers before? Because I don't see them here. Where are your glasses? The light is green now, ugh!"

Anna started talking to our daughter.

"Anyway ... How is my honey doing?"

Our daughter said, "I'm doing go—"

"I don't know where the papers are," Tony said. "I can't believe we are Face Timing in the car, HA HA! How is my honey? Did you show her the car?"

This proceeded until they arrived home, at which point we were all treated to a play-by-play of them trying to find the keys—which Tony had somehow misplaced on his way from the car to the door—to open the door. When they finally arrived inside, the call switched to Wi-Fi and subsequently froze.

The Man in the Garlic Tuxedo

Tony is somewhat wary of social media; however, he does recognize its importance from a business standpoint. Therefore, he set up a Twitter account for his business.

My guess is that he started to feel as though he was acclimating himself quite well to Twitter[79], and thus gained the confidence to set up his own personal Twitter account.

The following are a sampling of tweets Tony has sent forth into the Internet stratosphere from said account. As a means of providing a background on his grasp of Twitter, I will say that Tony once uttered the phrase "Donald Trump accepted my submission to receive his tweets." Not quite sure what that meant, but it probably had something to do with this:

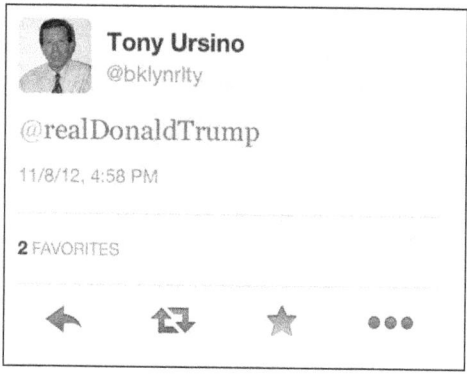

This is a tweet at Donald Trump with no text. There's an excellent chance someone got fired just because this tweet exists.

---

[79] He tweeted twice from his business account, but he locked his account so no one can read the tweets. The account is following nobody and has zero followers.

The Greatest Communicator

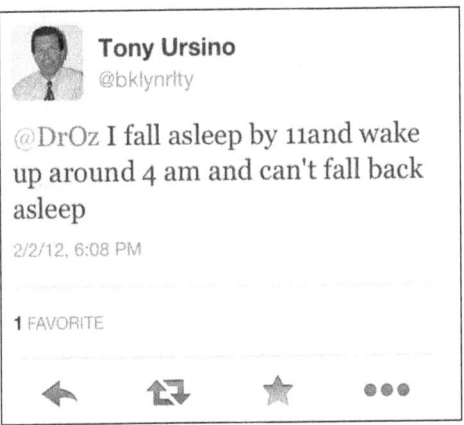

This is a tweet at Dr. Oz. Unfortunately, Dr. Oz did not respond to Tony's health problem on Twitter. Thanks a lot, Dr. Oz, you jerkhead! I'm fairly certain my father-in-law joined Twitter for the sole purpose of making this statement, and you don't even have the courtesy to respond? How the hell is he supposed to fall back asleep when the television doctor he solicits on the Internet doesn't bother to get back with an answer? For shame.

The Man in the Garlic Tuxedo

This is a tweet at me, Anthony, Matt, and my sister-in-law Maureen, a failed reply to a tweet Anthony had sent after we booked a holiday family vacation in Colorado. Again, there is no text. For those unfamiliar with Twitter, this is the equivalent of yelling, "Yo, Mike, Ant, Matt, Maureen!" and then saying nothing else. Thankfully, Tony followed up that mistake with a general tweet to everyone.

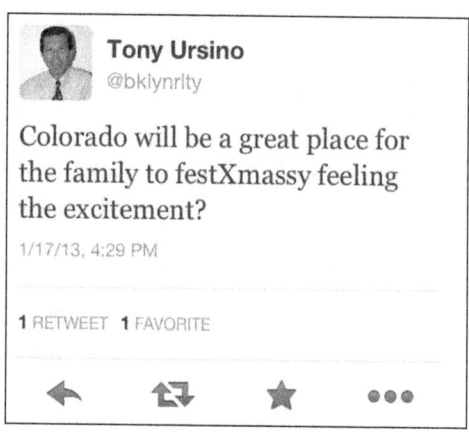

The retweet on that was Anthony and the favorite was mine (all the favorites are mine), and the lack of additional responses indicates that, unfortunately, no—no one else was feeling the excitement.

Well, I guess *we* were feeling the excitement. We tried to have T-shirts made just for this family vacation that read "#festXmassy" on the front and "feeling the excitement?" on the back, but most of our family didn't get the joke and didn't want to fork over $20 for a T-shirt they didn't understand.

But festXmassy is immortal and can never be forgotten. One day festXmassy will trend on Twitter.

That is my life goal.

The Philosopher

Text from me to Anthony:

> Your dad to your sister last night at dinner: "There are two things that are the most important things in life, the two things more important than anything. The first is your husband. The second is your feet."

Listen—there's an ancient, uh, Indian proverb, and it goes … "Walk a mile in some moccasins … " No, it goes, "You can't … before you say ANYTHING, you need to walk in another man's moccasins." I think you guys need to walk in MY moccasins to see how I'm feeling right now. Because then you'd know I am PISSED OFF. Just think about that. And you guys, heh—you guys better finish the job the

right way because if you don't ... I'll know. Believe me I'll know. Mike, give me the keys!

Those were the words of my father-in-law before leaving to meet my wife at the car dealership. He was dropping that knowledge on two electricians with bad attitudes who had just cut holes into our garage wall in an attempt to fix an electrical problem caused by the recent installation of our solar panels. Tony was in rare form on this day—or, more accurately, he was in usual form—and his moccasin metaphor and heightened state of emotion should have sent out a bat signal to all local car dealers: "Beware. This man is coming to see you now."

As I stood there in the garage with two men I didn't know, who my father-in-law had just yelled at before peeling off—a strangely familiar position for me—I was comforted by the fact that at least he'd be on time to meet Monica. We had plans for dinner with friends in a matter of hours, and I knew she was very stressed that he wouldn't show up when he'd promised based on his long and storied history of never doing that. The night before Tony had told her not to worry—in fact, the structure of their car deal was already in place thanks to an hours-long trip to the dealership a few days prior. Tony just had "a few more questions" for the salesman.

The salesman had actually called Monica several times during the previous few days to see where they stood on the deal; however, she was under strict orders not to speak to him directly. Therefore, the worst-case scenario would have been Monica arriving at the dealership before her dad, and either wasting precious time waiting in her car or risk blowing the whole deal by speaking without him present.

The Philosopher

Shortly after Tony left, my mother-in-law arrived at our house to give me a hand with our daughter. After a while, Anna received a text from her own daughter that read:

> I am here. Where is dad? When did he leave? PLEASE TELL ME HE LEFT!

How was he not there? He had left forty-five minutes earlier, and the place was only fifteen minutes away. Anna called her husband. He was at the car dealership ... technically.

Tony was at the Honda dealership across the street from Subaru. He was pretending to be interested in purchasing a comparable Honda so he could get some numbers to leverage a better deal than he had already tentatively agreed to with the Subaru dealer. When Anna called him, he was in the presence of two salesmen and the sales manager sipping—surprise—a cup of coffee. He would later admit that in that moment, he had already gotten the numbers he wanted, but was in too deep and unsure how to escape. Honda was basically getting paperwork ready for him to sign when he somehow weaseled his way out of there.

Monica was obviously thrilled to find out her dad was at another car dealership pretending to buy a different car, but once he finally arrived—and he has such a way of doing this no matter how late he is—he immediately put her angst at bay by getting right down to business.

I have already mentioned how prone he is to taking cell phone calls while in the middle of something else. Well, during this particular time Hurricane Sandy had just dilapidated a great portion of the East Coast, including Brooklyn. That entire week Tony was fielding desperate calls from displaced homeowners and tenants looking for a place to stay. It was really taking a toll on him emotionally, hearing the horror stories. Anyway, being smack dab in the middle of intense car negotiations and doing so under time constraints did not dissuade him from taking calls. I later received this text from my wife:

> Leaving Subaru soon with dad … he's fielding calls from hurricane victims for apartments for rent and making deals … He's unstoppable! Looks like we have a deal.

Tony was in the zone. According to Monica, it was an unprecedented display, even by his own standards, of negotiation and multitasking. After being presented with the deal they had tentatively agreed to just days earlier, Tony shook his head condescendingly and asked the salesman, "Do you believe in God?"

Do you believe in God?

The question shook my wife to the core of her being. It was quite a big matzo ball to throw out there, and she was horrified her father had asked such a question and dreaded the salesman's response. Thankfully for everyone involved, over the course of hours that spanned several days, the Subaru salesman had come to develop an understanding, albeit limited, of how Tony operates. It may be a stretch to say he appreciated Tony's style, but he bore no outward indication of despising it. He handled my father-in-law's existential question with as much aplomb as a car salesperson can and responded, "I do. But even He wouldn't forgive me for this interest rate."

The Philosopher

It was such a fantastic response that Tony's attention was diverted from explaining his purpose for the question in the first place. After hearing the account of the proceedings I personally was *very* interested in discovering the meaning of his original question. My interrogation, however, proved futile since by that point Tony already had to be reminded he had even posed the question. In Tony's reality, things like asking a car salesman if he believes in God are just things that happen throughout the course of a given day and require no further reflection.

When all was said and done, and the Subaru dealer had affirmed his faith in an omnipotent being, Monica's monthly payment was reduced by another thirty dollars compared to the original offer. She also received a bunch of other incentives including free oil changes and an extended warranty.

That night we drove my wife's new car out to meet friends for dinner while my in-laws babysat. When we returned home, my mother-in-law was watching the Food Network in complete darkness other than the flicker of the TV as her husband lay sprawled and passed out next to her on the couch after a long day of fighting other people's battles.

After about five minutes of going over the events of the evening with Anna, Tony suddenly popped up, looked at the TV—which in his most recent state of consciousness was on the Golf Channel—and said, "Where's golf? Let's go," and stumbled to the door like a drunk person leaving a bar.

As I chuckled watching him leave our house, Anna scrambling to trail him, I looked down and noticed he was wearing what could easily be described as moccasins. I quickly determined he must be the only person who could walk in them.

The Tough Mudder

My buddy Pete sent me an email that the Tough Mudder was coming to Phoenix. Although he had already completed several, he said he would come out to Arizona for this one if I committed. Sure, I was in. Why not? It was just a twelve-mile adventure mud run featuring twenty-five-plus obstacles including electrical shocks and something called the "Arctic Enema." What was the big deal?

I knew my in-laws and Anthony would be in Arizona during that time, so Pete and I figured we'd get a team together. Anthony was in, as was Tony, although I doubt he really understood what he was committing to. You can pretty much ask my father-in-law to do anything and he will say yes ... and then the day before the event he will openly wonder what he got himself into and ask you a million questions, all of which have been answered previously in various emails[80] he ignored and phone conversations during which he was not paying attention.

"Hey, Dad, a bunch of us are going to enter an event where we dress like clowns and hang glide over the Grand Canyon and then ride a banana boat down the Colorado River. You in? It's $1,000 each."

"Yeah, sure, whatever. Register for me and remind me when it gets close."

Sure enough, a few days before the Tough Mudder, Tony finally looked at a map of the course online and was like, "Wait ... *what?*" He wasn't by any means backing down, but he finally became aware that this was not a run-of-the-mill race where he could get by on sheer Italianism and his willpower to remain young. I mean, Anthony and I were concerned how *we'd* get through it, and our combined ages didn't equal Tony's.

We had to climb a twelve-foot wall just to get into the starting corral. From there we were warned that several people had already suffered broken bones and oh—one person had a heart attack. Armed with that information, we were off, and you can guess who led the way.[81]

The Arctic Enema was the third obstacle. It featured a dumpster filled with ice water and a piece of plywood in the

---

[80] It should be mentioned, however, that during email correspondence that attempted to collectively determine our team name, Tony excitedly submitted "FORCE FLEX." It was, umm, not the name we chose.

[81] The entire theme of Tough Mudder is teamwork, and staying with your team, and not leaving anyone behind, but Tony ran ahead of us the entire time. Of course we reconnected at each obstacle, but he simply could not remain with us during the running portion. It's obvious that it's physically impossible for him to run adjacent to a loved one.

The Tough Mudder

middle. In order to get to the other side, you had to fully submerge yourself in freezing water and go under the plywood. It was pretty much the worst thing ever. For Tony, it was nothing more than a chilly, refreshing bath. In fact, the person behind Tony in the dumpster began yelling at him because Tony was taking too long to get out. He might as well have been doing the backstroke in there.

From there we jumped gorges, crawled through tubes of mud, jumped off fifteen-foot high platforms into more freezing water, carried heavy wooden logs for what seemed like miles, and climbed various structures, all while soaking wet and/or muddy and exhausted. The final obstacle was "Electro Shock Therapy," which featured dangling live wires hanging over mud. We had kinda sorta promised Anna that we wouldn't let Tony do that one, but ... you know. At that point it wasn't like we were going to skip the last obstacle, and we did everything as a team.

It was awful. Crawling through that mud and hearing the piercing *sssssssnAP* sound of a shockwave zapping someone, followed by a painful yelp was psychologically taxing. Actually *getting* shocked was much, much worse. Anthony tried to walk instead of crawl and got dropped immediately like a ton of bricks. I took one to the back that was so powerful it reverberated to Pete, who was crawling next to me. In front of us was Tony, who was absorbing shocks left and right but moving forward nonetheless. As our fearless leader, he trudged ahead, never forgetting to yell back important advice like "Watch out guys! For the wir—OWWWAHHHH!"

When we finished, all four of us were predictably spent. I, however, was shivering uncontrollably to the point of being

The Man in the Garlic Tuxedo

unable to hold the main prize for finishing, a beer. My three teammates got a kick out of this, especially my father-in-law. There he was, this sixty-three-year-old man covered in mud after just having completed an event created for meathead college kids and young adults, laughing at me for being unable to stop shaking.

Tony's joy at finishing the Tough Mudder, especially as part of a team of much younger men, was palpable. He wore a crafty, proud smile the remainder of the day, and it didn't take a psychic to read his mind.

Yep. Still got it.

The Enigma

Part of the reason it is so supremely difficult to describe my father-in-law is that many of the things he does defy explanation. It becomes increasingly complicated when one considers that many of the things he does that initially *appear* to defy explanation often do have an explanation—a very good and useful one, in fact. Yet anyone who knows him on a level exceeding that of mere acquaintance knows Tony's uncanny ability to do utterly mystifying things.

What's more—what makes these occasions so bewildering—is that they are so insignificant in nature. They are random happenings, the nonsensical daily exploits of an otherwise supremely intelligent, street-smart man.

There was the time Anthony went to Lowe's with his dad to pick up light bulbs and batteries for his new place. They were at the self-checkout line, and as Anthony began scanning the barcode on the items, Tony decided to help his son by getting a plastic bag.

As anyone who has ever been to a self-checkout knows, the bags are right there. Literally they are *right there.* If you do nothing except scan the item and place it on the adjacent surface, there is a chance it will fall *into a bag.* Anthony's station was not out of bags. There were plenty of bags. Thousands of bags. Right there. When Tony said he was "going to get a plastic bag," Anthony was already confused because: Why would he verbalize that instead of just reaching out his arm and grabbing one right now?

Indeed, Tony was "going" to get a plastic bag in that he went to a different self-checkout station at which a woman was innocently scanning and bagging her own items. Without saying anything, Tony sidled up next to her—Anthony remains unsure if he pushed/nudged her out of the way, but he's pretty sure shoulders touched—*removed the bag she was using,* placed it down, and grabbed a fresh plastic bag from her allotment of plastic bags.

When Anthony turned around to see what the heck his dad was doing and where he even went, he saw a look of disgust on the woman's face that is typically reserved for encounters with the worst types of criminals. This woman was seething with disdain for Anthony's father because his father had done something extremely socially awkward for no apparent reason. There is no doubt this woman went home and immediately told anyone with ears about this weird encounter while using rhetorical phrases like "What is this world coming to?"

Had this been an isolated incident of bizarre behavior, a

sense of embarrassment for what his father had done may have come over Anthony, but that ship had sailed long ago. Instead, Anthony just laughed. As Tony walked back across the aisle he smiled, happy that his son was laughing, although he wasn't sure why his son was laughing, and happy that he had retrieved a plastic bag as promised.

When Anthony arrived home he texted me right away to tell me what happened, and then *I* was happy, too.

Not that I haven't had my own direct encounters with The Enigma.

Tony was driving us to the tennis courts. It was strange we were driving at all since the courts are a three-minute walk from his house, but he wanted to drive for a reason known only to him. This is not what confused me, although it *was* confusing.

He parked the car in the lot facing the courts, in an end spot in front of a wide, grassy median. On that grassy median the sprinklers were active.

Because we were in the end spot, my path was pretty clear to the courts. I simply needed to exit and walk straight toward the courts, remaining on asphalt the whole time, which is what I did.

Something, some kind of sixth sense borne of knowing him for more than a decade, told me that Tony was going to walk through the sprinklers. Still, my logical side informed me that he would just go around the car to my side, avoiding the water spray.

That was not what happened, which was both surprising and unsurprising. There I stood, safe and dry on the edge of the parking lot, watching my father-in-law walk through the sprinklers for no reason. He awkwardly juggled everything he was holding in an attempt to not get it wet—his phone, racket, sleeve of balls, other phone, towel, keys. Yet he was in no rush whatsoever. He was not scurrying; he was moving at a slower than normal pace. Water was splashing him in the face and body. Even better, instead of moving straight through the sprinklers or veering to his right to where the median narrowed—which, by the way, would have been a much more direct route to the courts—he veered to his left, where the median widened, absorbing more direct water hits.

He had a weird look on his face, too. It was a smirk that suggested he knew what he was doing, but with a strong hint of embarrassment, as if he couldn't believe what he had just done. It was a look that said, "Did I do this on purpose or by mistake? Even I don't know. All I know is, the slower I go, the better."

When he arrived back on asphalt soaking wet, I had no words. I just smiled at him and shook my head, and he smiled back. I thought what I always think on such occasions: I have to text Anthony.

The Environmentalist

Being from the East Coast, it never ceases to seem silly to us when winter weather warnings reach Arizona. These warnings, however, are not without merit, as pipes can freeze and plants can die. I realize that is not as dramatic as extreme blizzards, but the point is—it *does* get cold.

Such a winter weather warning came through while my in-laws were in the desert for their usual extended January visit. In fact, it seemed as though this was going to be the most extreme cold to hit the desert since Monica and I had moved there, and some precautions were necessary. Specifically, cover your plants and your outdoor exposed pipes.

I was curious as to how Tony would react to these warnings since he takes particular delight in not heeding warnings. I pictured him, experienced in all types of terrible East Coast weather through which he had traversed from New Jersey to Brooklyn and back against all rational advice, and imagined he would find humor in the idea of preparing for cold weather that would seem mild by comparison. I was surprised, however, by his willingness to participate. Just a few months prior, Hurricane Sandy had hit the Northeast, and I think it sparked in Tony a newfound respect for Mother Nature. Also, the fact that there were frost delays on the golf courses for his morning tee times reiterated the urgency of the incoming cold. If it was starting to affect his *golf*, then this was serious.

The day before the real cold was slated to hit, Tony helped me cover the pipes. Then he went home to cover his own water pipes as I brought most of our potted plants into the garage to keep them safe. The rest of our outdoor plant life would need to be covered, but we didn't have enough old sheets and blankets to cover everything.

Luckily for us, when Tony returned he came bearing gifts. A fitted bedsheet and half of a window curtain. "Hooray, we are saved!" Monica and I said sarcastically. He stressed that the most important thing was that we cover the lemon tree. It was imperative that the lemon tree stay warm and safe. WE CANNOT LOSE THE LEMONS AND ALL OF THEIR HEALTH BENEFITS. I agreed, so I grabbed the ladder and we went outside to cover the tree.

Once we were outside, Tony handed me the bedsheet he had brought. I looked at it, looked at the tree, looked at the sheet again, and this happened:

"Dad," I said, "uh, I don't think this is going to fit."

"What? Pfft, sure it will fit. Look at it."

Tony opened the bedsheet, revealing exactly how small it was compared to the tree.

"I don't know, Dad—I mean, this tree is kind of big."

"It stretches out, this sheet, so if you stretch it the way you're supposed to, it will fit. Trust me. It might be too big, actually."

"I guess covering some of it is better than none of it."

"I think this will cover all of it."

I tried to drape the sheet over the lemon tree, but kept getting punctured by the tree's thorns.

"Make sure you stretch it out," Tony said. "Did you stretch it out enough?"

"I'm trying … ow!"

"Be careful. The lemon tree has thorns."

"Thanks."

"Make sure you get the branch there. You have to stretch it."

"I'm stretching it as much as I can. I don't think it has any stretch left."

"Did you stretch it?"

"I'm just … I'm trying."

"You definitely have to stretch it, is the thing."

I was on the verge of losing my mind at this point and considered just jumping off the ladder into the thorny tree.

"I stretched it," I said. "It is stretched as far as it can go."

"Okay, okay. I think maybe it looks good. It looks like we covered everything from here. I told you it would fit."

I got down from the ladder.

"Are you sure?"

Mr. Self Aware

On my in-laws' coffee table rested a book titled *The Secret Language of Birthdays,* which was based on astrology and provided a detailed personality description for those born on each day of the calendar year.

We had all taken turns reading aloud the page about our respective birthday and what it said about our personality. We laughed at the anecdotes that seemed to perfectly describe us, and we laughed equally at the ones that did not. It was hit and miss, but it was interesting and funny to see how the book could pinpoint precise details of our character based on things like the moon and stars.

Eventually it was Tony's turn. He was skeptical, and so was I. How could a book describe the indescribable man?[82] Tony had to be coerced by the rest of us to read his May 27

---

[82] Yes, I get the contradiction of that sentence.

The Man in the Garlic Tuxedo

page, and he did so reluctantly, the words read with the force and volume of a passing breeze, drenched in skepticism.

He began:

"'The Day of Driven Dedication.[83]

"'Not ones to be silent in general, they state their opinion in sharp, outspoken terms.

"'May 27 people often have a wild and wacky view of the world. Indeed, their zany sense of humor can cause consternation, as they are not averse to sharing their thoughts whenever moved to do so.

"'It is less a lack of tact or diplomacy but rather poor timing which can put others off.

"'Whether outrageous personalities or conservative ones, those born on this day exercise great influence on others, but the reactions they provoke are often bewildering to them—consequently, they may end up completely ignoring what their critics have to say.'

"Pfft," Tony said. "That's just ... no." He continued, grudgingly.

"'So dedicated are May 27 people to what they do, that they can persevere for years with or without recognition, and thus stand a good chance of succeeding.

"'On the other hand, they can be blind to their shortcomings and often act as if they don't care.'

"Pfft," Tony said, again.

"'Typically those born on this day achieve their greatest success away from their birthplace, and they may feel the need

---

[83] Gary Goldschneider and Joost Elffers, *The Secret Language of Birthdays* (New York: Penguin, 1994), 214.

Mr. Self Aware

to travel to other localities, where they become adopted citizens.'"

Tony removed his glasses, put the book down, and said, "This is not to be believed."

The rest of us sat wide-eyed and slack-jawed. One page of one book had pretty much nailed it.

I apologize you've had to read so much of this book to get here, but I thought some specifics might help.

Babbo Part Two

It has been a remarkable thing to witness, the transformation from Tony to Babbo. It has astounded me, no doubt, but Monica—raised under the iron curtain of discipline—has found it nearly impossible. From her perspective, strictly in the matter of his role as patriarch, he is a completely different person, one she often doesn't recognize.

Easter morning 2012, we all waited outside a breakfast restaurant after church in the increasingly warm Arizona sun. Our daughter was midway through a "refusing to eat without a fight" phase, and part of our remedy at that time was the elimination of most treats, especially before mealtimes. My father-in-law was holding her, and after about three seconds of waiting impatiently outside, he ventured with her back indoors to the hostess stand to try to work his magic. He re-emerged saying, "We're next," and our daughter was holding and happily licking an absurdly gigantic yellow lollipop.

"DAD!" Monica said. "Are you kidding me?"

Monica took the lollipop out of our daughter's hand. Our daughter flipped out.

"You know she's not supposed to have this," Monica said, "and we're gonna eat in like two minutes."

Our daughter continued flipping out.

"What?" Tony said. "She said she wanted it."

"I'm sorry," Monica said. "SHE SAID SHE WANTED IT? When in my entire life did I ever get something because *(air quotes)* 'I wanted it'? You once deprived me of dessert for two weeks because I didn't finish the last bite of the PIG LIVER you forced us to eat, and she gets a lollipop because 'she wanted it'? No. Uh uh."

Our daughter had flipped out to the point where I had to take her from Tony's arms and remove her from the public sphere.

"I don't know," Tony said to Monica. "Maybe you should just relax."

I ran with the child for safety.

Now, Tony is Babbo twice over.

Our second daughter came to us via foster care in spring 2013. We adopted her that summer, and again my in-laws were there for the court hearing. The judge, who was great, made it a point to thank our supporters in attendance, especially my in-laws, to whom she made a special acknowledgment. My father-in-law, under the impression this was a cue to say a few words, stood and said, "I am Tony, the father of

Babbo Part Two

the moth—" before being interrupted by the judge, who had continued with the proceedings. Again, she was great.

Like her sister before her, our other little one is mildly obsessed with her Babbo. This could be because the second time she "met" him was, not surprisingly, via FaceTime, and during the call Tony managed to get his foot stuck in the spindle of his coffee table. It caused quite a scene, and all conversation was put on hold so Anna could get Tony's foot removed from the coffee table while our younger daughter, then two, looked on in amazement from miles away.

"Ha, ha … you funny, Babbo!" she said over and over again, even though Babbo was not laughing but wincing in foot pain, which she considered all part of the show.

Now every time they talk she asks him how his foot is doing, and he proves his foot is doing just fine by pointing the phone's camera on his bare foot for minutes at a time. "You want to count my toes, honey?" he will ask. "One … two …" but she went to play with toys five minutes ago.

"Dad, it's me," I'll say. "I see your bunions."

The *first* time my in-laws met their newest grandchild also occurred with the help of FaceTime. We called them thinking they were home, but when the call connected we were treated to a view of an anonymous paneled ceiling and my father-in-law negotiating the price of a circular saw. They were at the hardware store, but Tony decided to answer the call anyway.

"Guys, we can call you back," Monica and I insisted, but Anna instead took the phone and moved to a quiet aisle in the hardware store where we could share this moving, intimate family moment. Then, in the background, we heard Tony say, "Hold on, Bill—I just have to meet my new granddaughter, but I do want to talk more about that price. We're not finished talking yet, okay, Bill?"

"Oh, 'Glenn,' yeah that's right, Glenn. Sorry about that."

My Father-in-Law

While my own family was getting bigger, Tony and Anna now had an empty nest, and figured it was time to downgrade.

They moved into a smaller home in an adjacent New Jersey suburb. A beautiful home for sure, but not bereft of the various issues that face all incoming homeowners—the ones missed during inspection.

It was around this time when they were settling in that I was having frequent conversations with Tony for his input on this very book. We were scheduled to meet via FaceTime to go over some details, but when I called it was Anna who answered.

She told me that unfortunately our talk for that evening would have to be postponed because Tony was "outside trying to get mice out of the drainage pipe."

According to my mother-in-law, Tony had set up quite

a contraption in the efforts of driving the mice out of the drainage pipe. The contraption was several broomstick handles held together with electrical tape. It was pouring rain as Tony jammed the broomstick contraption down the drainage pipe.

I wondered about the merits of this plan since it seemed the broomstick contraption would work well if there were one fat mouse that was stuck in the pipe as opposed to several mice that were living in the pipe. Was he trying to *scrape* them out? It remains uncertain, and it also did not work.

No matter, however, because by the time I had called, Tony was already on to phase two.

The Juicy Fruit phase.

Tony had lined up sticks of Juicy Fruit gum near the end of the drainage pipe in an effort to convince the mice to come out and feast. Utilizing yet another home remedy of sorts, Tony had learned via urban legend that mice cannot digest Juicy Fruit gum and, unable to release feces, will spontaneously combust in to tiny mice parts. While I talked to Anna, Tony was on a stakeout in a dry spot under the roof, waiting for the mice to come out and take the bait. This is why he could not talk.

Alas, phase two also did not work. The whole ordeal was very Elmer Fudd-ish, and eventually, to Tony's great chagrin, a pest control professional had to be contacted. He arrived armed with packs of Juicy Fruit strapped to his chest like Rambo. Just kidding—he arrived with actual mice-removal things, and Tony followed him around the entire time to make sure he was doing it right.

It was okay, I assured Anna, that Tony couldn't come to

the phone. Even though we didn't talk, I now had more to write.

And so it was with this book. I would think that I had everything written, and then Tony would go and walk through the sprinklers, or give toddler-size ice skates to his adult son, or, when asked if he'd like to hear the specials, say to a kind waitress, "You are from Egypt" (and be right).

Other than being its subject, Tony was very far removed from the process of writing this book. I asked him if I could write it, I talked to him about it as I began, and I clued him in as to the themes and anecdotes. Eventually, after writing many pages based solely on my direct personal experiences, I needed to sit down with him and get some details from his past. Then and only then did he finally realize I was writing a book about him.

"Wait, you're really doing this?"

The fact that he has yet to comprehend why I did this is, in itself, a reason I wanted to do this. Everything he does, good or bad, comes from a genuineness that I deem to be so rare. To sit back and watch him is to observe a man who could care less that you are watching him. In fact, he wasn't even listening when you told him you'd be taking notes. He exists, in many ways, in his own world, resistant to the idea that anyone would have even the faintest interest in his day-to-day life. Tony is who he is in a way that is so undeniably pure because he rarely if ever corrupts himself by pondering who he is in the eyes of others.

The Man in the Garlic Tuxedo

Years ago Monica provided detailed instructions about meeting her father, but it is now "someday," and she was right—I do understand. So much so that this is, I guess, the instruction manual.

Tony is many, many things, I have come to learn, and surely I will learn more considering it took Anthony twenty-plus years to find out his dad was a Greek-speaking carpenter. To me, however, there is but one descriptor that will suffice. Tony is my father-in-law.

For that, I am truly blessed. My preconceived notions about what my in-laws and brothers-in-law might be like proved comically inaccurate, although—thanks to a self-proclaimed captain—we've never lacked for comedy.

Or advice, or direction, or confusion, or assistance, or interference, or breakfast, lunch, and dinner, or home remedies, or unsolicited and undesired commentary, or faith, or hope.

Or love.

Thanks again, chicken.

Acknowledgements

This is a book about one man, Tony, but it's really about family. As such, I have mostly my family to thank.

First and foremost the man himself, who allowed me to do this and never once sought to hinder my progress. It takes a big man to give someone free rein to write his memoir, and Tony is a big man and a good sport, and, for those reasons and many others, my favorite muse.

My wife who, being the offspring of this book's subject, allowed this to be possible in the first place. She also helped me immensely with this project in very tangible ways, including providing the idea for the cover; utilizing her uncanny memory to provide the details of her and her brothers' upbringing; fact checking for accuracy; and generally acting as my sounding board for the past few years as this book developed. She is my toughest critic, and I love her for it (and for many, many other reasons).

The Man in the Garlic Tuxedo

My personal team of amateur ragtag editors and very biased observers, included my wife, mom, brother-in-law Anthony, and our dear family friend Robert, a.k.a. Cib, a.k.a. Professor Brilliant. My mom would print out various drafts of the manuscript, make copious notes, and then lose everything. Anthony would build me up, telling me everything was great and that he loved it. (He also did some serious pro bono guerilla marketing, like bringing up my blog page on twenty computers before running out of the Apple store.) Professor Brilliant, a.k.a. the Comma Nazi, would then bring me back down to Earth with his deadpan delivery of criticism—"Stop using 'like.' Are you some kind of valley girl?"—and gushing praise—"This is okay." It provided a healthy, strangely perfect dynamic, and I owe them all my gratitude and maybe a gift card or something.

My dad who, besides always providing great feedback on all my writing—"Yeah I read it ..." —was totally cool with his son writing a book about his father-in-law instead of his own father. Rest assured, *The Deacon Who Mysteriously Lost All His Phone Apps and Needs Help Getting Them Back* is already in the works. (It is not, but I still love and admire the heck out of ya, Dad.)

Anna, whose input and unique perspective was crucial to this book. One day she will be known as the patron saint of May 27th husbands, and one of the three miracles that will occur after her passing many, many years from now will be when an angel wearing red underwear visits Kohl's.

Joe and Matt, for everything they provided in their own right and for agreeing to be a part of this whole thing. If someone told me I was going to appear in a book but my

Acknowledgements

legacy in said book would be the time I accidentally farted in a Canadian restaurant or the time my crotch almost caught fire, I'm not sure I would agree to those terms. They are greater men than I am.

To my sisters, Kelly and Jill, for allowing me to reveal their respective celiac disease and sensitive nature. I just realized I never technically asked either of them if that would be okay, sooooooooo, hopefully that was cool? Guess I'll find out when I see them on Thanksgiving. On *gluten-free* Thanksgiving.

To my daughters, who I fear may read this years from now and ask why I didn't thank them. Thank you, girls—I couldn't have done this without you!

To everyone mentioned in these pages: thank you, I love you, and also I am sorry.

A great big thank you to everyone at The Editorial Department, especially Jane ("Janey," "Juana") Ryder, Christoper ("C-Dog") Fisher, Morgana ("The Irish Flutist") Gallaway, Catherine the Design Queen, Amanda ("The Hammer") Bauch, and Peter Gelfan ("Peter Gelfan"), whose help, support, and encouragement made this process memorable, fun and, for the most part, stress free. Thank you to Mark Korsak for the amazing cover design. (And thank you to Auburn McCanta for introducing me to these wonderful folks.) If anyone out there is considering publishing a book, it is my estimation that you will do no better than The Editorial Department.

I maintain a genuine sense of awe for how God allows things to unfold. When I sit back and think about what life was like just fifteen years ago, it's fascinating to consider every seemingly minor event that brought together everyone mentioned in these pages. Thank you, God Almighty, for blessing

The Man in the Garlic Tuxedo

me with this family—the one I was born into, the one I was married into, and the one we are trying like heck to raise right now—my own modest trinity that is really one. Thank you for giving me the ability to string words together somewhat coherently, and thus welcome in anyone and everyone who would like to be a part of this lovable dysfunction.

And thank *you* for reading this, and thus choosing to do so.

If you'd like to read more, check out the blog at mikekenny.blogspot.com (and validate its existence by liking it on Facebook), or follow me on Twitter, @mikekennystuff. Email me your spam or just to say "hi" at mikekenny.stuff@gmail.com.

www.ingramcontent.com/pod-product-compliance
Lightning Source LLC
Chambersburg PA
CBHW030635150426
42811CB00077B/2109/J